DROPPED STITCHES

—IN—

TENNESSEE HISTORY

———

—BY—

JOHN ALLISON

———

The Overmountain Press

JOHNSON CITY, TENNESSEE

Original Copyright © 1897
by John Allison
Reprinted 1991 by The Overmountain Press
ISBN 0-932807-52-6
Printed in the United States of America

DEDICATION

To the Memory of My Mother,

WHO, WHEN I WAS BUT A YOUTH,

FIRST INTERESTED ME IN AND TAUGHT ME MUCH

OF THE

EARLY HISTORY

OF THE

PIONEERS OF MY NATIVE STATE.

PREFACE.

THIS little volume, as will appear to the reader, is not a history of anything nor of anybody, and is not so intended. The whole is simply an effort to put together in readable form some facts in the very earliest history of Tennessee not hitherto fully shown, if even mentioned.

I was born and brought up at Jonesboro, in Washington county, Tennessee, and resided there until 1889.

My mother, when I was a mere boy, first interested me in and taught me much about the pioneers and early history of my native state. Following up much learned from her, I frequently visited old gentlemen and aged ladies in Eastern Tennessee and a few in North Carolina, and conversed with them about "old times" and their early lives, and from them obtained much information not to be gotten in any other way. By a formal order of the County Court of Washington county, made many years ago, I was given custody and possession of the very earliest court records made at Jonesboro (records from 1778 up to 1800, as I now remember), and had possession of them for two or three years, and at odd times went through and copied much from these old records. I had, however, become interested in, and read much, from these court records before the order of the court giving me possession of them.

I made, as best I could, original investigation as to facts plainly suggested by the proceedings of the courts, as to the men who constituted the court, their lives, character, etc., and also as to the events surrounding, or involved in, the entries as indicated by the substance of the "motions," "orders," etc.

Where authorities consulted and information obtained in my original investigation have conflicted as to a date, I have given that which seemed most probably the correct one; where no date at all could be found or fixed, I have followed the "illustrious example of distinguished historians," and said, "about this time"—without giving any date at all.

By permission of my long, long time scholarly friend, Dr. R. L. C. White, the author, I publish with the volume "A Centennial Dream" with the Key thereto. The "dream" and interpretation are put in an appendix, for the reason that I can not copyright either.

Dr. White's "Centennial Dream" has suggested, in fewer words, more Tennessee history than any publication heretofore made, and, as hundreds of persons can testify, has excited more interest, and caused more thorough investigation, in Early History of Tennessee, than any book or paper hitherto written on the subject. It will live as an attractive, proficient instructor and teacher of the history of the "Volunteer State" after he has "crossed over the river" and is at "rest under the shade of the trees."

All who read the dream and key to it will appreciate the obligation I am under to Dr. White.

CONTENTS

DROPPED STITCHES

——IN——

TENNESSEE HISTORY

CHAPTER I.

ANDREW JACKSON, ATTORNEY AT LAW.

MOST English-reading people, as well as many of those who read history written in other languages, are familiar with the life and deeds of *General* and *President* Andrew Jackson; and very many people in the United States know of *Senator* and *Judge* Andrew Jackson. Few, however, are acquainted with young Andrew Jackson, Esq., attorney at law, of Jonesboro, then (1788–9) the county-seat of Washington county, North Carolina. They are all one and the same personage; and it can truthfully be said that there is a still smaller number who know anything whatever about the leading and dominating characteristics of the people among whom young Andrew Jackson really began life, at Jonesboro, in what is now Washington county, Tennessee.

Most of Jackson's biographers, and nearly all of those who have written and spoken about him, make him begin his business and professional life at Nashville, in the fall of the year 1788. John Reid, in his "Life of Andrew Jackson" (published in 1817), says that Jackson, on reaching the settlement on the Holston river, near Jonesboro, remained there until October, 1788, when he left and went to Nashville, arriving at the latter

place during the same month. Jenkins, in his " Life of General Jackson " (published in 1850), says that Jackson reached
Nashville in October, 1788.   Parton, in his " Life of Jackson"
(published in 1860), says: " Upon the settlement of the difficulties between North Carolina and her western counties (1788),
John McNairy, a friend of Jackson's, was appointed judge of
the Superior Court for the Western District, and Jackson was
invested with the office of solicitor or prosecutor for the same
district. . . . . Thomas Searcy, another of Jackson's
friends, received the appointment of clerk of the court. . . .
Before the end of October, 1788, the long train of immigrants,
among whom was Mr. Solicitor Jackson, reached Nashville, to
the great joy of the settlers there. "

The distinguished historians are all in error in all of these
statements.   There was no Superior Court at Nashville at this
date.   The act of the general assembly of North Carolina, providing for or establishing a Superior Court of Law and Equity
for the counties of Davidson, Sumner and Tennessee, was not
passed until November, 1788.   The act passed at Fayetteville,
in that month, "erected the counties of Davidson, Sumner and
Tennessee into a district for the holding of Superior Courts of
Law and Equity therein, by the name of Mero. " The first
volume of the original record of the minutes of the Superior
Court of Law and Equity for the district of Washington—then
the "Western District"—at Jonesboro, shows that David
Campbell alone held that court from the February term, 1788
(which was the first term), until the February term, 1789, at
which latter term the record shows that Judge McNairy appeared
and sat with Judge Campbell.   The same volume shows that,
at the February term, 1788, and on the first day of the term,
Francis Alexander Ramsey was appointed and qualified as clerk
of the court, and that "Archibald Roan was appointed Attorney

to prosecute on behalf of the State," on the first day of the term, but that he resigned on the following day; "whereupon, William Sharp, Esq. is appointed in his room." Sharp continued to act as prosecuting attorney until February, 1790, when, as the record shows, he was succeeded by William Cocke. The same volume has this entry: "August Term 1788. John McNairy Esq. produced a License to practice as an Attorney in the several Courts within this State with a certificate from the Clerk of the Court for the District of Salisbury that he has taken the oaths necessary for his qualification as an attorney whereupon he is admitted to Practice in this Court."

The Superior Court of Law and Equity for the Mero District was not formally organized and opened until late in the year 1789, when John McNairy was appointed judge of that court.

Under the territorial form of government provided by Congress, in May, 1790, for "the territory of the United States of America south of the river Ohio," the President appointed three attorneys for the territory—one for Washington District, one for Hamilton District and one for the "Mero District." Andrew Jackson was appointed in and for the "District of Mero," and I have not been able to find any evidence whatever that he held any office whatever prior to this appointment. It is doubtful whether he ever received any compensation from the government of the United States for the services rendered as attorney of the "Mero District;" for, at the first session of the third general assembly of Tennessee, an act was passed, October 26, 1799, the second section of which is as follows: "Be it enacted, that the sum of four hundred dollars shall be and the same is hereby appropriated for the payment of the sum due Andrew Jackson, as a full compensation for his services as Attorney General for the District of Mero under the territorial government." Andrew Jackson never accepted payment twice for the same service.

Section 1 of the same act appropriates two hundred dollars "to Archibald Roane, as full compensation for services as Attorney General for the District of Hamilton under the territorial government."

Jackson did not arrive at Nashville until the fall of the year 1789 or the spring of 1790—most probably the latter. He "settled" in Jonesboro, in what was then Washington county, North Carolina, and is now Washington county, Tennessee, in the early part of the spring of 1788. He probably came from Morganton, North Carolina, across the range of mountains to Jonesboro, as early in the spring as the melting snow and ice made such a trip over the Appalachians possible. From Morganton to Jonesboro, by the trail or route then travelled, was more than one hundred miles, two-thirds of which, at that time, was without a single human habitation along its course. As emigration from east of the mountains to "the new world west of the Alleghanies" was considerable about this period, it is quite possible that Judge McNairy and others came at the same time; but who they all were, and the exact date of their arrival in Jonesboro, is not known.

On the old record books of the minutes of the proceedings of the Court of Pleas and Quarter Sessions kept at Jonesboro will be found the following entry: "State of North Carolina Washington County, Monday the Twelfth day of May Anno Domini One Thousand Seven Hundred and Eighty Eight. Andrew Jackson Esq. came into Court and Produced a license as an Attorney With A Certificate sufficiently Attested of his Taking the Oaths Necessary to said office and Was admitted to Practiss as an Attorney in this County Court." The entry immediately preceding recites that "Archibald Roane, David Allison, and

Joseph Hamilton Esquires Produced sufficient Licenses to Practiss as Attorneys and were admitted," etc. ; and the entry immediately following recites that "John McNairey Produced a license as an Attorney," etc., and "was admitted to Practiss as an attorney," etc.

Thus this old record shows the admission to the bar, on the same day, in the one-story log court-house, twenty-four feet square, at Jonesboro, of five young men.

Jackson's promotion from one office to another, until he reached the highest and most exalted office on earth, the Presidency of the United States, is known to all; but that " Twelfth day of May Anno Domini One Thousand Seven Hundred and Eighty Eight " must have been a lucky day, or there must have been good material in those young men—for Andrew Jackson was not the only one of them who attained eminence.   Jackson was first United States attorney for the " District of Mero," but Roane held the same office at the same time in the Hamilton District, while McNairy presided over both of them as federal judge for "the territory of the United States of America south of the river Ohio."   Jackson met both McNairy and Roane as fellow delegates in the constitutional convention for Tennessee, in 1796.   Jackson was afterward a judge of the Superior Court of Law and Equity, but so were both McNairy and Roane—and this, too, before Jackson reached the bench, they having been elected at the first session of the first general assembly of Tennessee, in April, 1796, before the state had been formally admitted into the Union by act of Congress. Their decisions, however, were never called into question on that ground.

In 1797, McNairy was appointed a district judge of the Federal Court in Tennessee, which position he held continuously until his death in 1831 or 1832, leaving his reputation as a wise and just judge and an upright man as a heritage to Tennesseans.

Roane resigned his judgeship in June, 1801, and was elected Governor of Tennessee in the following August. On retiring from the office of Governor, after having served two years, he remained in private life until 1811, when he was appointed circuit judge. Thereafter—in October, 1815—he was again appointed to the Superior Court bench, where he remained until April or May, 1818, and then retired from public service, honored and esteemed.

David Allison was commissioned "Master of the Rolls and Clerk in Equity of the Superior Court of Law and Equity" for Washington District at Jonesboro, by Judges Samuel Spencer and David Campbell, in August, 1788. He held this office for about two years, resigning in 1790, when he went to the settlement on the Cumberland—now Nashville—and engaged, I believe, in the mercantile business.

Joseph Hamilton disappears entirely from the court records and proceedings at Jonesboro, and I have been able only to trace him elsewhere, as Clerk of the County Court of Caswell county, State of Franklin, 1785, and when he was appointed by the territorial Governor and Council to aid in running and marking the lines of Knox and Jefferson counties, when they were established in 1792, and where he was appointed one of the Trustees of Greeneville College in 1794.

It was while Roane was Governor, in 1802, that the memorable contest between John Sevier and Andrew Jackson, for the position of Major General of militia in Tennessee, occurred. It was no empty and meaningless honor to hold this position then in the state—as subsequent events demonstrated. Under the terms of the constitution, the Major General was elected by the field officers of the militia. When the votes which had

been cast were counted, there was found to be a tie between
Jackson and Sevier.   The Governor, by virtue of his office,
was commander-in-chief of the militia.   He was therefore a
field officer, and as such was entitled to cast, and did cast, the
deciding vote between these two great commanders.   Governor
Roane gave his vote for Jackson, and Jackson thus became
Major General of militia in Tennessee, which led him up to the
victory he gained over the British at New Orleans, and this
victory eventually made him President of the United States.
If Roane had voted for Sevier?— I am a Presbyterian.

Roane was a candidate for re-election to the office of Governor, in August, 1803.   John Sevier was a candidate against
him, and defeated him, notwithstanding the fact that Roane
had the earnest and active support of Jackson.   Jackson and
Roane combined could not beat Sevier before the people,
although the latter had been three times Governor theretofore.
Roane, as before stated, remained in private life until 1811.
Sevier was twice elected Governor after having defeated Roane,
and remained in public service almost continuously until his
death in September, 1815.   To give in detail the various
offices with which John Sevier was honored, every one of
which he honored in turn, would be foreign to the subject.   He
filled every office known to the statutes—and some which were
unknown—except two: he was never a Senator in Congress
nor a judge of any of the Superior Courts.   (He was not a
lawyer.)   Nothing that could be said on the subject would add
to this evidence of the confidence the people had in him, and
of their faith in and affection for the man.

Jackson had attained to the age of twenty-one years on the
15th of March preceding the entry above quoted, admitting
him to the bar in Washington county.   He may have been
formally admitted at Salisbury or Morganton, North Carolina,

but he did not in fact open an office or enter upon the practice
of law at either place.   The order admitting him to the bar at
Jonesboro, therefore, may be accepted and regarded as the
opening entry in the business life and the professional and
political career of this, one of the greatest of all Americans.

These old court records at Jonesboro disclose the fact that
Jackson was in the town and in attendance on the Court of
Pleas and Quarter Sessions, at its November term, 1788.   Under the law at that time, bills of sale of slaves and horses and
deeds to land had to be proven in the court mentioned.   A
bill of sale was presented to this court by Jackson, at its
November term, 1788.   This bill of sale is given below, for
reasons hereafter to be stated.   It is as follows: "A Bill of
Sale from Micajah Crews to Andrew Jackson, Esquire for A
Negroe Woman named Nancy about eighteen or twenty years
of Age was Proven in Open Court by the Oath of David Allison a Subscribing Witness and Ordered to be Recorded."

The court records for the years 1788 and 1789, kept in
Washington, Sullivan, Greene and Hawkins counties, establish
the fact that Jackson was practising law in those counties
during the two years mentioned.   He could not, in the very
nature of things, have attended court in those counties, if he
had been residing at Nashville or practising law in Davidson,
Sumner and Tennessee counties, which at that time constituted
the " District of Mero."

It has been stated without qualification by some writers that
Jackson was present in Morganton, North Carolina, when Governor John Sevier escaped from the authorities there and returned
to "the western waters."   Parton says that "Jackson may have
witnessed the celebrated rescue of Governor Sevier, as, about
the time of its occurrence in 1788, he was at Morganton, on a
visit to Colonel Waightstill Avery, on his way to the western

wilds of Tennessee." Sevier, for having organized and been elected Governor of the "lost state of Franklin," was arrested near Jonesboro, in October, 1788, and taken to Morganton; but there was no such "celebrated rescue" or escape of Sevier as that pictured in the various accounts of this affair which have been given. Sevier, on reaching Morganton, was met by Generals Charles McDowell and Joseph McDowell, who became his bondsmen until he could make a visit to a brother-in-law who resided some miles from the town. Sevier made this visit, returning to Morganton on the second day after leaving, and reported to the sheriff of Burke county, who permitted him to go where he pleased without requiring bond. In the meantime, Sevier's two sons, James and John, together with Major Evans, Mr. Crosby and probably others from "the western waters," had arrived in Morganton; and, in consequence of what was then told to Sevier by his sons and friends (which need not be stated here), he left Morganton, quietly and openly, in broad day, and returned with them immediately to Washington county. All of these occurrences took place during the month of October, 1788; and Jackson could not have been, during this month, in Morganton, in Jonesboro and in Nashville. He was, as before stated, at Jonesboro, familiarizing himself with the country and getting acquainted with the people in the counties mentioned.

It has been written of Jackson that he came into the "new settlements" on foot, or that he walked from Morganton to Jonesboro. This is incorrect. More than twenty-five years ago, the writer made it his business to investigate the truth of that statement, and also other incidents and facts in reference to the early life of Jackson while he made his home at Jonesboro. There were then living in Washington and the surrounding counties several aged native-born citizens who had known

Jackson personally, and who had heard much concerning him. These old gentlemen, who ranged in age around eighty-five years, delighted to talk of what they knew and had heard of Jackson when he came to Jonesboro, and while he lived there during the years 1788 and 1789. All that has been or will be stated herein is from notes of conversations had with them, and either taken literally from or based on the old court records at Jonesboro. From these sources of information it can be asserted as truth that Jackson arrived in Jonesboro riding one horse and leading another; that the horse he was riding was a ''race horse;'' that he had a pair of '' holsters'' (pistols) buckled across the front of his saddle; and that on the led horse was a shot gun, a '' pack'' and a well-filled pair of saddle-bags, while following after him and by his side was a goodly pack of foxhounds. This is an inventory of his personal belongings, as given me by at least three of these old gentlemen, * each of whom had known Jackson personally, and had heard the story of his arrival in the community repeated often by fathers, mothers and others. It is reasonable to infer that he had some money also, or he could not, within a few months after his arrival, have purchased the slave shown, by the bill of sale set out above, to have been bought by him. The price of such a slave as that described was at that time about three hundred dollars. When one of the old gentlemen referred to was told by me that it had been said and '' published '' that Jackson had come to Jonesboro '' afoot,'' he fired up and his eyes fairly sparkled as he exclaimed: '' Good God! Jackson never walked anywhere from necessity. He came here riding a race-horse and leading another first-rate horse.''

Jackson made his home, while he remained in the eastern

---

* Major Bird Brown, Abram Taylor and John Allison.

RESIDENCE OF CHRISTOPHER TAYLOR.

Where Andrew Jackson boarded during years 1788-9. Showing port-holes. Erected about 1773. From a photograph taken in April, 1897.

part of what is now Tennessee, at the house of Christopher Taylor (father of Abram Taylor, before mentioned), about one mile west of Jonesboro, on the road that led from the town to the "Brown settlement" on the Nolichucky river. The old house is still standing, and can be seen from the passing trains on the Southern railway. A view of it, as it appeared some years ago, is given.

Christopher Taylor was a slaveholder and a large landowner, and had some race-horses which were fairly good for the times, together with a pack of the "finest and fastest hounds" in the country. While every one knew that Jackson was a devotee of the race-course, a lover of the chase and not averse to a cock-fight, still he was admired and esteemed by all, from the time he came into the country.

It is not probable that he had a law-office in Jonesboro, the tradition being that he received and consulted with his clients at Christopher Taylor's, when court was not in session. When he was consulted by a client, his first effort was to compromise or adjust the difference, if possible; failing in this, he was most stubborn and unrelenting on behalf of his client, never, however, resorting to anything not in keeping with the strictest rules of propriety and fairness, and always courteous, manly and open in his bearing toward court, jury and opposing counsel, and exacting from every one the most respectful and courteous treatment, whether in court, at the race-course or elsewhere. He never insinuated anything—he spoke it out plainly. He despised deceit and treachery, and he held in the highest esteem the bold, open loyalty of a man to a friend or a conviction. He loathed any man who was guilty of a little mean, or mean little, act. He had a profound contempt for the narrow-minded and penurious or niggardly man. He himself was not extravagant, but his heart and hand seemed to open sponta-

neously to a deserving object of charity. Strange to say, while
he did not know what fear was, he was often heard to express
great sympathy for cowards or the timid, and he would never
allow such an one to be imposed on in his presence.

It is not necessary to recite evidence or narrate circumstances
to show that such a man as Jackson had the most exalted opinion of woman, and that he was always her champion and de-
fender; but an incident which occurred at Rogersville, in Hawkins county, will be related here. A most estimable widow
kept the "tavern" at Rogersville. Her house was generally
full during court week. One day, a stranger came into the
public or reception room, shortly before supper, and asked for
entertainment or a room. The landlady in person showed him
a room, with two or three beds in it, and told him that he
could, if he wished, occupy that room with two other gentlemen, having a bed to himself, explaining that, on account of
it being court week, her house was so crowded that she could
not give him a separate room. The stranger was not pleased
with this arrangement, and so told the landlady. As they returned to the public room, the stranger, just as they entered it,
made some insolent remark about a country and a town which
could not afford a gentleman a separate room. Jackson, who
was sitting in the room, heard the remark. Springing to his
feet, he seized the stranger by the arm, exclaiming, "Come
with me, sir—I'll find a separate room and bed for you!" The
stranger, observing Jackson's tone and manner, hesitated, and
asked him what he meant. The only answer he received was,
"Come on, sir!" and he reluctantly went with Jackson, who
was still holding him by the arm. Jackson took his captive
out the "back way," and brought him up in front of a corn-
crib, in which were some corn and shucks. Opening the door
of the crib, he commanded the stranger to "climb in," at the

same time displaying in his right hand an argument that so overcame all desire of resistance that prompt obedience was the immediate result.   The stranger "climbed in," apologizing and begging at the same time, and Jackson closed the door upon him.   After looking at his prisoner for some minutes with great satisfaction, Jackson asked him if he was willing to go back to the house, apologize to the landlady, and accept the room which she had offered him.   The stranger readily expressed his willingness to do this, which he did, and so the incident closed.

In going from Jonesboro to the courts in Greene, Hawkins and Sullivan counties, Jackson always took with him his shotgun, holsters and saddlebags, and very often his hounds, so that he was always ready to join in a deer chase or a fox hunt. He was an unerring marksman, and was always the centre of attraction at the "shooting matches," at which the prizes were quarters of beef, turkeys and deer.   He would dismount anywhere on these trips, in order to participate in such a contest; and messengers were frequently sent from remote parts of the settlements, inviting him to come out and join in a hunt or a "shooting match."   He invariably accepted such invitations.

In those early days, when a new settler came into the community, or a young man married, as soon as the place for the "clearing" and the erection of a cabin was fixed upon, the neighbors "gathered in," and they had what was called a "house raising" and a "barn raising."   They felled the trees, hewed the logs and built the house and barn—all in one day, or in two days at most.   It was said that Jackson attended more of these house and barn "raisings" than any other one man in the country.   They usually wound up with a fox hunt, a deer chase or a shooting match.   He was said to have been "a horseman without an equal, the boldest and most fearless

rider⌷that had ever crossed the Alleghanies." He would ford
or swim his horse through a river wherever he came to it, if he
wished to get to the opposite side. His aggressiveness and
restlessness were often the subject of remark, and led to the
opinion, which was freely expressed, that if ever there was a
war, he would be a great general.

He began life among people who had views and opinions of
their own on all questions of the day and subjects of public interest; yet his judgment was consulted and his views sought on
almost all public affairs, notwithstanding his youth. He was
recognized from the first as a man who "would fight at the drop
of a hat, and drop the hat himself"; but in all the personal
difficulties which he had while he resided in Washington county,
save one—a duel with Col. Avery, an account of which will be
given in another chapter—public opinion was generally largely
in his favor.

It may, and it should, be interesting to those who love and
revere the memory of Andrew Jackson to know something of
the life, habits and characteristics of the people among whom
he first settled at Jonesboro, as well as of those with whom he
afterwards made his permanent home at Nashville; for whatever can be said to the credit and glory of either the early settlers on the Watauga or those upon the Cumberland can be
truthfully said of the others. Therefore, a brief account of the
dominating characteristics of the people among whom he first
settled will be given. This will, it is believed, throw some light
on the formation of Jackson's character, methods and course
throughout his life.

CHAPTER II.

THE PICKETS OF CIVILIZATION.

THE first settlers in Tennessee: what did they do?

They founded and administered the first free and independent government in America. They established the first church, the first institution of learning, and the second newspaper, in "the new world west of the Alleghanies."

They were in the wilderness. The hour of the day was determined by the shadow cast by the sun upon the home-made dial; the time of the night was reckoned from the positions of particular stars in the firmament. Years and months they measured by moons. From the course, color and velocity of clouds, from the temperature and from the direction of the winds, they foretold the weather. They also observed the habits of animals and birds of passage, as aids to their weather bureau; and they watched and studied closely the development and growth of plants, herbs, vines, vegetables and the cereals, as helps to their agricultural department.*

The country in which Andrew Jackson made his home for about two years deserves a name and place in history not yet fully given to it. In its wild and picturesque magnificence, in the rugged honesty and frank simplicity of the people who settled it, in their love and struggle for liberty, "home rule" and local self-government, it was a counterpart of the Switzerland of tradition and story.

The sun shone nowhere upon a land of more ravishing loveliness and awe-inspiring sublimity—silver threads of river and

---

* The almanac-groundhog and goose-bone theories were adopted by a later and wiser generation.

streamlet, and gem of valley set in emerald of gorgeous luxuri-
ance; waters murmuring and thunderous, striking every note
in the gamut of nature's weird minstrelsy, dashing and bound-
ing to the sea; every acclivity a Niagara of color flashing from
rhododendron and mountain magnolia, elysian fields without
Rhenish castles or Roman towers; grooved with fastnesses, ter-
raced with plateaus and monumented with peaks upheaved
into a very dreamland of beauty and grandeur, all overlooked
by the majestic Roan—

> " The monarch of mountains—
> They crowned him long ago,
> On a throne of rock, in a robe of clouds,
> With a diadem of snow! "

About one hundred and thirty years ago, the first permanent
white settlement was made on the Watauga river, near where
Elizabethton now stands. Up to the winter of 1770–1, there
were in all probability twenty families in the new settlement.

May 16, 1771, the "Regulators" fought the famous but disastrous battle of the Alamance, about forty miles northwest of
Raleigh. During the summer and fall following this battle,
settlers came in considerable numbers to "the new world west
of the Alleghanies," and cast their lot with the settlers on the
Watauga; and about this time settlements were made on the
Holston and Nolichucky rivers.

Who were these people? Whence and why did they come?
I answer:

They were every one patriots, soldiers and good citizens.
They came from the battlefield of the Alamance—that first contest of the revolution which eventuated in American independence. They left their homes because of the disastrous result
of that battle, in which many of them had participated, and because of their unconquerable hatred of the British government

and their open revolt against British authority and the oppression of British officials.

The following letter from Hon. George Bancroft, the historian, then Minister from the United States to Great Britain, on the subject of the "Mecklenburg Resolves," and the subsequent course and conduct of some of those engaged in the battle of the Alamance, is still of great interest to Tennesseans:

90 EATON PLACE, LONDON, July 4, 1848.

MY DEAR SIR—I hold it of good augury that your letter of the 12th of June reached me by the Herman just in time to be answered this morning. You may be sure that I have spared no pains to discover the Resolves of the Committee of Mecklenburg. A glance at the map will show you that in those days the traffic in that part of North Carolina took a southerly direction, and people in Charleston, and sometimes in Savannah, knew what was going on in 'Charlotte Town' before Gov. Martin. The first account of the Resolves extraordinary, ' by the people in Charlotte Town, Mecklenburg County,' was sent over by Sir James Wright, then Governor of Georgia, in a letter of the 20th of June, 1775. The newspaper thus transmitted is still preserved, and is the number 498 of the South Carolina Gazette and Country Journal, Tuesday, June 13, 1775. I read the Resolves, you may be sure, with reverence, and immediately obtained a copy of them, thinking myself the sole discoverer. I do not send you the copy, as it is identically the same with the paper you enclosed to me, but I forward to you a transcript of the entire letter of Sir James Wright. The newspapers seem to have reached him after he had finished his dispatch, for the paragraph relating to it is added in his own handwriting, the former part being written by a secretary. I have read a great many papers relating to the Regulators, and am having copies made of a large number. Your own state ought to have them all, and the expense would be, for the state, insignificant, if it does not send an agent on purpose. A few hundred dollars would copy all you need from the State Paper Office on all North Carolina topics. The Regulators are on many accounts important. They form the connecting link between the resistance to the Stamp Act and the movement of 1775, and they also played a glorious part in taking possession of the Mississippi Valley, toward which they were irresistibly carried by their love of independence. It is a mistake if any

2

have supposed that the Regulators were cowed down by their defeat at Alamance.   Like the mammoth, they shook the bolt from their brow and crossed the mountains.

I shall always be glad to hear from you and to be of use to you or your State.   Very truly yours,

GEORGE BANCROFT.

D. L. SWAIN, ESQ., Chapel Hill, N. C.

One of the "ringleaders" in organizing the Regulators for the battle of the Alamance was John Pugh, who was afterwards sheriff of Washington county, which at that time included all of the territory now embraced within the boundaries of the state of Tennessee.   Among the few names of the participants in the battle of the Alamance which have been preserved in history may be found those of several who were afterwards prominent among the settlers on Watauga, Holston and Nolichucky.   I have said this much because of some facts which will be given further along.

These people were on the very verge of the frontier, standing as a mere handful of pickets out on the confines of civilization, where the war-whoop of the painted savage rang through the forests, and the constant apprehension of the tomahawk and the scalping-knife haunted every abode, and every thicket ambushed a bloodthirsty foe.   When open daring failed, fiendish cunning, the torch and midnight butchery wrought the ruin. Atrocity followed atrocity, in the utter extinction of homes. Men hunted, fished, toiled, slept and worshipped with their trusty rifles at hand.   The women also, through necessity and with courage inspired by constant peril, were no less dextrous in the use of deadly weapons, and no less unerring in the precision of their aim.   The very genius of evil and desolation seemed at times to brood over the infant settlements.   Still, they prospered; and, amid their dangers, they followed industrial pursuits.   The creaking clang of the loom and the whir

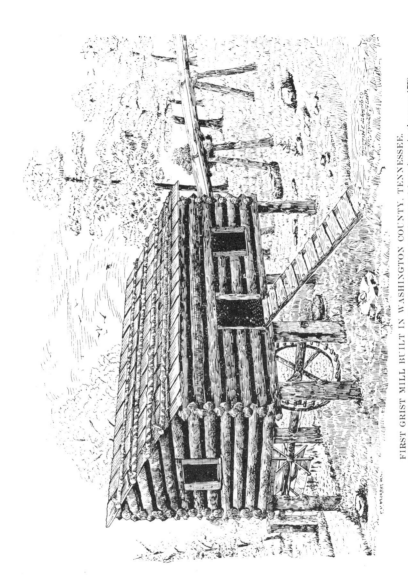

FIRST GRIST MILL BUILT IN WASHINGTON COUNTY, TENNESSEE.

Erected by Michael Bacon, on Little Limestone Creek, six miles southwest of Jonesboro, in the year 1779.

of the spinning-wheel furnished the "accompaniment to the maiden's concord of measured monotones." The woodman's axe felled the forest trees, and fields and farms were opened up, fenced and put in cultivation. Churches and schools were established, and public highways "viewed out" and opened up in the wilderness.

Among the wealthiest the wheaten cake appeared only at the Sabbath breakfast. Milk and spring water were their only drinks at meals. The red deer flitted through the voiceless solitudes, and bruin roamed the jungles at will. The fruits of the chase and the fishing-rod, together with pounded maize, supplied the wholesome comforts of the hospitable board. Quilting bees, log rollings, house raisings, corn shuckings, flax pullings, maple sugar boilings and the innocent abandon of the dance, enlivened with brimming gourds of nectared dew and the high fun and mirth of backwoods "social functions," gave variety and zest to the monotony of frontier life.

Maid and matron were clad in fabrics of their own handi-work, each a Joan of Arc in moral and physical prowess and power, and a Venus in rounded symmetry and development, with all the unaffected graces of natural and unspoiled womanhood, "the red wine of lusty life mantling and blushing in the ala-baster face"; the men garbed in skins or the coarsest textures of the loom, athletic of limb and fleet of foot as the roe, more than a match for all the cunning stratagems of Indian warfare, "lion-hearted to dare and win, and yet with gentleness and generosity to melt the soul."

The log structure rose in the wilderness, with puncheon floor, slab benches, port-hole windows and rifle-rack, in whose cribbed and darkened shrine alternated the thunderous vociferations of the fire-and-brimstone preacher and the cries of the truant urchin under the savage birch of the pitiless schoolmaster.

These people were without any local form of civil government, without executive, military, civil or peace officers; but they had among them John Sevier, Isaac Shelby, James Robertson and others, who kept the good of the community at heart.   It will be remembered that there has been much controversy, at times in the not very distant past, as to when, where and by whom the first declaration of a free and independent government was made and entered into on this continent—some claiming that Mecklenburg, North Carolina, was the place, its citizens the people, and May, 1775, the date; others asserting that the association formed for Kentucky, "under the great elm tree outside the fort at Boonsboro"—this also in 1775—was the first. I propose to show that neither one of these associations, declarations or formations of government was the first "free and independent government" established on this continent; but that this honor belongs to the settlers on the Watauga.   Haywood, in his history of Tennessee (page 41), says: "In 1772 (May), the settlement on the Watauga, being without government, formed a written association and articles for their conduct. They appointed five commissioners, a majority of whom was to decide all matters of controversy, and to govern and direct for the common good in other respects"; and again (page 46): "This committee settled all private controversies, and had a clerk, Felix Walker, now or lately a member of Congress from North Carolina.   They had also a sheriff.   This committee had stated and regular times for holding their sessions, and took the laws of Virginia for the standard of decision."   Haywood further says that they were living under this government in November, 1775.

Some four years after this local, self, independent government had been entered into by the settlers of Watauga, John Sevier, in a memorial to the North Carolina legislature explaining it, says: "Finding ourselves on the frontiers, and being apprehensive that, for want of a proper legislature, we might become a shelter for such as endeavor to defraud their creditors; considering also the necessity of recording deeds, wills, and doing other public business, we, by consent of the people, formed a court for the purposes above mentioned, taking, by desire of our constituents, the Virginia laws for our guide, so near as the situation of affairs would permit. This was intended for ourselves, and was done by consent of every individual."

I rather suspect that some inquiry was made by the authorities of North Carolina, as to what kind of a government this was which had been set up within their jurisdiction, and which established courts that took the laws of *Virginia* as their guide.

The "written association and articles for their conduct," entered into by the settlers on the Watauga, in May, 1772, formed the first "free and independent government" established and put into practical administration on this continent.

The five commissioners or committeemen first appointed were John Sevier, James Robertson, Charles Roberson, Zachariah Isbell and John Carter. This was an independent government, because they did not ask permission of any power on earth to enter into it, and they did not recognize any authority as superior to that which they had voluntarily vested in the five commissioners chosen by them. It was not a compact or league with any other power, but, as Sevier says, "was intended for ourselves." It was a free government, because it was voluntarily entered into by the whole people, "by consent of every individual."

The settlers lived, prospered and were happy, under the government of the five commissioners, for about six years. These commissioners settled all questions of debt, determined all rights of property, took the probate of wills and the acknowledgment

of deeds, recorded the same, issued marriage licenses and hanged
horse thieves, with much zest and great expedition—the ar-
raignment, trial, conviction, condemnation and execution of a
horse thief all occurring within an hour or so after he was arrested, inasmuch as they had no jail in which to imprison him
overnight, and believed strongly in the idea that a man who was
bad enough to be put in jail deserved to be hanged on the spot.

In November, 1777, the assembly of North Carolina erected the
District of Washington into Washington county, which included
the whole of what is now the state of Tennessee.   This was the
first territorial division in the United States named in honor of
George Washington.   The Governor of North Carolina appointed
justices of the peace and militia officers for this county, who,
in February, 1778, met and took the oath of office, and organized the new county and its courts.   Thereupon, the first ''free
and independent government'' formed and put into operation
in America was no more, the jurisdiction and authority of the
five commissioners having, by their own consent and that of the
people, been superseded by the newly appointed authorities.
The first written instrument, paper or record authoritatively
made in the organization of what is today the judicial, political, civil and military existence of the state of Tennessee, is
in the office of the county clerk at Jonesboro, and is in the
words and figures following:

FEBRUARY COURT 1778

The oaths of the Justices of the peace melitia & for officers
There Attestments, &c,

Washington County, I A. B. do solemnly swear that as a
Justice of the peace, and a Justice of the County Court of
pleas, & Quarter Sessions in the County of Washington, in all
articles in the Commission to me directed.   I will do equal
Right to the poor and to the Rich to the Best of my Judgment
and according to the Law of the State.   I will not privately or
Openly by my-self or any other person, be of Council in any

Quarrel, or Suit, depending Before me, and I will hold the County Court, and Quarter Sessions of my County, as the Statue in that case shall and may direct.

The fines and amerciaments that shall happen to be maid and the forfeitures that shall be incurred I will cause to be duly entered without Concealment. I will not wittingly or willingly take by myself or any Other Person, for me, any fee, Gift, Gratuity, or reward whatsoever for any matter or thing by me to be done, By virtue of my office except such fees as are or may be directed or Limited by statue, but well and truly I will do my office, of a Justice of the peace as well within the County Court of pleas, and Quarter Sessions as without. I will not delay person of common Right, By reason of any Letter, or order from any person or persons in authority to me directed, or per any other Cause whatever, and if any Letter or Order Come to me, contrary to Law I will proceed to Inforce the Law, such letter or Order notwithstanding. I will not direct or cause to be directed any warrent by me to be maid to the parties. But will direct all such Warrants to the Sheriff or Constable of, the County or Other the Officers, Of the State or Other Indiferant person to do execution Thereof, and finally, in all things belonging to my office, during Continuation therein will faithfully, Truly and Justly according to the best of my (Jud) skill and Judgment do equal and Impartial Justice to the Public and to Individuals, So help me God. Jas, Robertson, Valentine Sevier, John Carter, John Sevier, Jacob Womack, Robert Lucas, Andr, Greer, John Shelby Jr, George Russill, William Been, Zacr. Isbell, Jno McNabb, Tho, Houghton, William Clark, Jno McMaihen, Benjamin Gist, J. Chisholm, Joseph Wilson, William Cobb, James Stuart, Michl, Woods, Richd. White, Benjamin Wilson, Charles Roberson, William McNabb, Thos Price, Jesse Walton.

This oath has a deep and significant meaning, in view of the practices which had characterized the administration of justice by British officials. It is worthy of note that this oath, so full and specific in detail, did not bind those who took it to allegiance either to the state or the colony of North Carolina, or to the United States of America. It did bind them, however, to be honest, just and faithful to the people; it did bind them to "do equal right to the poor and to the rich"; it did bind them not to make suggestions or give counsel in any quarrel or suit pending before them, not to delay any person in obtaining justice, not to allow outside influence to dictate or control their actions, not to accept any fee, gift, gratuity or reward whatsoever for any matter or thing by them to be done, except the compensation allowed by law; to keep an account of fines and to enter them without concealment; and, finally, to "do equal and impartial justice to the public and to individuals." This oath was not merely administered to them in the modern, perfunctory way, as "You do solemnly swear," etc. They *took* it, repeated it after the officer, and signed it.

The new order of things was an innovation on the former simple, direct and expeditious way of administering justice; but the five "committeemen" were also members of the new court, and methods were not very materially changed, as the records of the clerk's office at Jonesboro will show. They took jurisdiction of all matters relating to the public good, and disposed of all questions summarily, as will be more fully and particularly shown in another chapter.

Whenever a stranger appeared in the settlements, and gave his name as William Morningstar, Samuel Sunshine or Walter Rainbow, he would not be there long before he would be waited upon by a committee, one of whom would say to him: "Look here, stranger, we have examined the book of Genesis from end to end since you came here, and we can't find the name of your ancestors. We think that you have got another name, and that you stole a horse somewhere and have run off. You must leave this settlement before night, or we'll hang you!" Such frank treatment was invariably effective: its object was sure to heed the warning and to disappear before sunrise the next morning.

About this time a vigorous and ambitious young man left the city of Philadelphia for the wilds of the southwest. His mind was stored with the rich intellectual treasures of old

THE FIRST CHURCH AND FIRST SCHOOLHOUSE BUILT IN THE "NEW WORLD WEST OF THE ALLEGHANIES." Afterward, and now, Washington College and Old Salem Church. The picture is an exact reproduction of the original log house, with log partition, erected by Samuel Doak, D.D., 1780, eight miles southwest of Jonesboro.

Princeton, then under the presidency of the father of Aaron Burr. He walked, driving before him through Delaware and Maryland, over the Alleghanies and across Virginia, his "flea-bitten grey," burdened to the utmost capacity with a huge sack of books. These classics were the nucleus of the library of an institution of learning yet unborn. After a fatiguing journey through a large portion of territory, with only obscure paths through gloomy forests for a highway, this devout and daunt-less adventurer halted among the settlers whom I have been describing. Soon thereafter, the first church—a Presbyterian —and the first institution of learning that were established west of the Alleghanies were founded. These were "Salem Church" and "Washington College," both established in the year 1780, eight miles southwest of the seat of the present town of Jonesboro—the college being the first one in the United States that honored itself by assuming the name of the Father of his Country. It is stated as a fact that, long prior to the late war, twenty-two members of the Congress of the United States had received or completed their education at Washing-ton College, under this pioneer in letters and religious training, whose achievements constitute the jewels of our early literary and moral history. This man was Rev. Samuel Doak, D.D. Though he left a deep and indelible impress on the civilization and the literature of the Southwest, he sleeps today, amid the scenes of his successful earthly labors, with only a simple and fast crumbling memorial to mark the hallowed sepulchre of his silent dust.

The settlers lived and their public affairs were conducted un-der the jurisdiction of the County Court of Pleas and Quarter Sessions for a period of about six years, in a quiet and orderly manner; but ever since that May day of 1772 when they organ-ized the first "free and independent government," their dream had been of a new, separate and independent commonwealth, and they began to be restless, dissatisfied and disaffected toward the government of North Carolina. Many causes seemed to conspire to increase their discontent. The first constitution of North Carolina had made provision for a future state within her limits, on the western side of the Alleghany mountains. The mother state had persistently refused, on the plea of poverty, to establish a Superior Court and appoint an attorney general or prosecuting officer for the inhabitants west of the mountains. In 1784, many claims for compensation for military services, supplies, etc., in the campaigns against the Indians, were presented to the state government from the settlements west of the Alleghanies. North Carolina was impoverished; and, notwithstanding the fact that these claims were just, reasonable and honest, it was suggested, and perhaps believed, ''that all pretences were laid hold of (by the settlers) to fabricate demands against the government, and that the industry and property of those who resided on the east side of the mountains were becoming the funds appropriated to discharge the debts contracted by those on the west.'' Thus it came about that, in May, 1784, North Carolina, in order to relieve herself of this burden, ceded to the United States her territory west of the Alleghanies, provided that Congress would accept it within two years. At a subsequent session, an act was passed retaining jurisdiction and sovereignty over the territory until it should have been accepted by Congress. Immediately after passing the act of cession, North Carolina closed the land office in the ceded territory, and nullified all entries of land made after May 25, 1784.

The passage of the cession act stopped the delivery of a quantity of goods which North Carolina was under promise to deliver to the Cherokee Indians, as compensation for their claim to certain lands. The failure to deliver these goods naturally exasperated the Cherokees, and caused them to commit depredations, from which the western settlers were of course the sufferers.

At this session, the North Carolina assembly, at Hillsboro, laid taxes, or assessed taxes and empowered Congress to collect them, and vested in Congress power to levy a duty on foreign merchandise.

The general opinion among the settlers west of the Alleghanies was that the territory would not be accepted by Congress (and in this they were correct); and that, for a period of two years, the people in that territory, being under the protection neither of the government of the United States nor of the state of North Carolina, would neither receive any support from abroad nor be able to command their own resources at home— for the North Carolina act had subjected them to the payment of taxes to the United States government. At the same time, there was no relaxation of Indian hostilities. Under these circumstances, the great body of the people west of the Alleghanies concluded that there was but one thing left for them to do, and that was to adopt a constitution and organize a state and a state government of their own. This they proceeded to do. Was there anything else which these people could have done? Perhaps there was; but did they not adopt just such a course as any people situated as they were would have taken?

They proceeded to take steps for the holding of a convention. Delegates were elected from Washington, Sullivan and Greene counties, who met in convention at Jonesboro, August 23, 1784. Messrs. Gocke, Outlaw, Carter, Campbell, Manifee, Martin, Roberson, Houston, Christian, Kennedy and Wilson were appointed a committee, ''to take under consideration the state of public affairs relative to the cession of the western country." This committee appointed Messrs. Cocke and Hardin a sub-committee to draft a report, which they did. This report was in the nature of an address to the people. The convention then adjourned, to meet again in Jonesboro, September 16. It did not, however, assemble on that date. In October, 1784, the North Carolina assembly repealed the act of cession. In the following November, the delegates again assembled at Jonesboro, but failed to adopt a constitution, and broke up in confusion, because of the repeal of the act of cession. John Sevier, having received official information that the cession act had been repealed, courts established, an attorney general appointed and military officers commissioned, made a speech advising the people to go no further; but Cocke and a majority of the people were unwilling to abandon their dream of a new state—and Sevier went with his people.

December 14, 1784, another convention assembled at Jonesboro, and adopted a constitution, which was to be ratified or rejected by a convention called to meet at Greeneville, November 14, 1785. In the meantime, a general assembly was elected, which met at Greeneville, early in 1785, and chose John Sevier for Governor, David Campbell judge of the Superior Court, and Joshua Gist and John Anderson assistant judges. Landon Carter was chosen Speaker of the Senate, and William Cage Speaker of the House. The same assembly, at the same session, afterward elected Landon Carter Secretary of State and William Cage State Treasurer. Joseph Hardin was then elected Speaker of the House, but I have not been able to ascertain from any source who was elected Speaker of the Senate in place of Carter. Stoakley Donaldson was made Surveyor General, and Daniel Kennedy and William Cocke were appointed Brigadiers General. The assembly elected all other officers, civil and military, being careful to choose those who

already held offices under the government of North Carolina—
and so the ill-starred "state of Franklin" began its career.
The new state was named in honor of Benjamin Franklin, as
the correspondence of Sevier conclusively shows, and the name
should therefore always be written "Franklin," and not
"Frankland."

The boundaries of the new state, as set forth in a paper in
the handwriting of Col. Arthur Campbell of Virginia, were as
follows: "Beginning at a point on the top of the Alleghany
or Appalachian mountains, so as a line drawn due north from
thence will touch the bank of the New river, otherwise called
Kenhawa, at the confluence of Little river, which is about one
mile above Ingle's ferry; down the said river Kenhawa to the
mouth of Rencovert or Greenbriar river; a direct line from
thence to the nearest summit of the Laurel mountain, and
along the highest part of the same to the point where it is in-
tersected by the parallel of thirty-seven degrees north latitude;
west along that latitude to a point where it is met by a meridian line that passes through the lower part of the rapids of
Ohio; south along the meridian to Elk river, a branch of the
Tennessee; down said river to its mouth, and down the Tennessee to the most southwardly part or bend in said river; a
direct line from thence to that branch of the Mobile called Donbigbee [Tombigbee]; down said river Donbigbee to its junction
with the Coosawatee river to the mouth of that branch of it
called the Higtower [Etowah]; thence south to the top of the
Appalachian mountains, or the highest land that divides the
sources of the eastern from the western waters; northwardly
along the middle of said heights and the top of the Appalachian mountains, to the beginning."

I am not prepared to say whether or not these people intended their new state to become part of the Union, as one of

the provisions in their proposed form of government was that
"the inhabitants within these limits agree with each other to
form themselves into a free, sovereign and independent body
politic or state, by the name of the commonwealth of Franklin." I am inclined to the opinion that in the beginning they
did not intend to join the Union of states, but that later they
concluded that they would, as there was an effort made to have
Congress recognize the new state.

An examination of the boundary lines of the state of Franklin will show that it included fifteen counties of Virginia, six
of West Virginia, one-third of Kentucky, one-half of Tennessee,
two-thirds of Alabama and more than one-fourth of Georgia.
Cast your eye over this magnificent area: see the blue mountains,
the sun-browned cliffs, the beautiful rivers, the broad valleys
with their golden wheat-fields and verdant meadows, with the
hundreds of smaller streams and sparkling springs: it seems
like one grand piece of natural embroidery, fashioned and put
together by the fingers of infinity and spread out by the hand
of the Almighty. Think of the iron, coal, marble, lead, cop-
per, zinc and other minerals hidden within its soil—you might
have put a Chinese wall around the people of the "state of
Franklin," and still they could have lived in absolute independence of the outside world. There is more iron and coal in this
territory than can be found in the same area elsewhere in the
United States, and it is today yielding a vast revenue to its inhabitants. You can stand on some of its mountain-tops, and
see the heavens darkened by day with the pillar of cloud, and
made luminous by night with the pillar of fire, arising from
furnace and forge in the valleys below, and hear the hammer
of Thor beating the iron ribs of those majestic old mountains
into the marvellous machines of modern invention and the util-
ities of a grand civilization.

At the first session of the general assembly of the state of Franklin, held in March, 1785, fifteen acts or laws were passed. In the act levying a tax for the support of the government was the following section:

Be it enacted, That it shall and may be lawful for the aforesaid land tax, and the free polls, to be paid in the following manner: Good flax linen, ten hundred, at three shillings and six pence per yard, Nine hundred at three shillings: Eight hundred two shillings and nine pence: Seven hundred two shillings and six pence: Six hundred two shillings: tow linen one shilling and nine pence: linsey three shillings: and woolen and cotton linsey three shillings and six pence per yard: Good clean beaver skin six shillings: cased Otter skins six shillings: uncased ditto five shillings: rackoon and fox skins one shilling and three pence: woolen cloth at ten shillings per yard: bacon well cured at six pence per pound: good clean beeswax one shilling per pound: good clean talow six pence per pound: good distilled rye whiskey at two shillings and six pence per gallon: good peach or apple brandy at three shillings per gallon: good country made sugar at one shilling per pound: deer skins, the pattern six shillings: good neat and well managed tobacco fit to be prized that may pass inspection the hundred, fifteen shillings, and so on in proportion for a greater or less quantity.

The last section of the act is in these words: "And all the salaries and allowances hereby made shall be paid by any treasurer, sheriff or collector of public taxes to any person entitled to the same, to be paid in specific articles as collected, and at the rates allowed by the state for the same, or in current money of the state of Franklin." This provision furnished those who adhered to the North Carolina government much amusement. They asserted that the salaries of the Governor, judges and other officers were to be paid in skins, absolutely; and, to add to their amusement, had them payable in mink skins at that. From this provision the inhabitants of that section of the country fell into the habit of referring to money as "mink skins;" and this term, as descriptive of money, thus spread all over the southwestern country.

They estimated by law two dollars and fifty cents to be equal to fifteen shillings of the current money of Franklin. They allowed the Governor two hundred pounds annually; the Attorney General twenty-five pounds for each court he attended; the Secretary of State twenty-five pounds and fees; the judge of the Superior Court one hundred and fifty pounds; the assistant judges twenty-five pounds for each court they attended; the treasurer forty pound; and each member of the council six shillings per day for each day of actual service.

A convention met in Greeneville, in November, 1785, to adopt a constitution. Up to this time no disagreement had taken place—all were for Franklin; but when the constitution which had been proposed was submitted, it was rejected; and, on motion of Col. William Cocke, the convention adopted the entire constitution of North Carolina. Thus began the trouble which ended in the overthrow of the state of Franklin.

I can not now notice the various sessions held by the assembly of Franklin. It met for the last time in Greeneville, in September, 1787. "During the years 1786 and 1787, a strange spectacle was presented—that of two empires being exercised at one and the same time, over one and the same territory and people." County courts were held in the same counties, under the Franklin and the North Carolina governments; "the same militia was called out by officers appointed by each government; laws were passed by both assemblies"; taxes were laid by authority of both states—but the people said that they did not know which government had the right to receive their taxes, and therefore they adopted the easy solution of paying to neither. The Superior Courts of Franklin were held at Jonesboro; the courts under North Carolina were held at Davis's on Buffalo creek, ten miles east of Jonesboro, and at Col. Tipton's. There were now two strong parties, one under Tipton, adhering to

HOUSE USED AS CAPITOL OF THE STATE OF FRANKLIN,
In Greeneville, Tennessee.   From a photograph taken in April, 1897.

North Carolina, and the friends of Franklin following Sevier, each of whom endeavored by every possible means to strengthen his cause. "Every provocation on the one side was surpassed in the way of retaliation by a still greater provocation on the other. . . . The clerks of the county courts of Washington, Greene and Sullivan, under Franklin, issued marriage licenses, and many persons were married by virtue of their authority."

In 1786, while a court was in session at Jonesboro, under the Franklin government, Col. John Tipton entered the court house with a party of men, took the records away from the clerk and drove the justices out of the house. Not long after this, Sevier entered the house where the North Carolina court was sitting, turned the justices out bodily and carried off the records. "The like acts were repeated several times during the existence of the Franklin government." James Sevier was clerk of Washington county under the Franklin government, as he had been under North Carolina. Tipton went to Sevier's house and took the old records away from him by force. Shortly afterward, the same records were recaptured, and James Sevier hid them in a cave. During these captures and removals many of the records were lost. Of the Franklin records all save one were either lost or destroyed.

This single remaining record of the Franklin courts is not only interesting but amusing; and, to be as drunk as it unquestionably is, contains some law and a great deal of early history. This record was evidently made late at night, by the light of a "tallow dip" or a bear-oil lamp, with a bottle of well-distilled apple or peach brandy near by. It is the only written record relative to the "lost state" and its courts that I have ever been able to find. It is like an old-time copy-book. On the outside are the following entries and memoranda—I give them literally:

3

State of Franklin,—Washington County
J James Sevier, State of Franklin James Sevier clerk of
Washington County State of Franklin
Franklin
Franklin
Franklin

Inside, in the same handwriting, will be found the following:

Good deeds are very commendable in youth,
Good many men of good many minds
Good birds of Good many kinds
State of ——————— Court Adg'd, till court In course
from a general insurrection of the times, to this date 7th, of
May 1786,

On the next page the record continues as follows:

Something ambiguous will say he went to the Indians, no
witnesses, no opportunity, they are not able to proove anything, The meaning is to be taken, the latter in contracts,
deeds and wills, construed differantly was there a ejectment,
and he never tryed, nothing can be done until Injunction issue
from the judge. The law says no party shall be tryed without
witnesses Hobgobblins, and Ghosts. So many tryals

Read and interpret this record in the flickering light of the
history of the times. The court had been broken up and the
justices driven out of the house—this, I suppose, is the "ejectment" referred to. John Sevier was at this time on the frontier,
fighting the Indians—hence, he "went to the Indians." There
was at this time in the hands of the North Carolina sheriff a
bench warrant for the arrest of Sevier; if he was arrested, the
charges against him could not be proven without witnesses;
these would be hard to procure against John Sevier, and yet no
one could be fairly "tryed without witnesses." So this clerk,
alone at midnight, with no company except the flask whose
odor seems still perceptible in the pages of his record, reasoned
and wrote—until the "Hobgobblins and Ghosts" got after him!

In January or February of 1788, John Sevier's property was
seized under a *fieri facias* issued by North Carolina. Sevier

and Tipton, with their respective followers, met and fought a slight battle two miles south of the present site of Johnson City, in which the former was repulsed. In the following October, Sevier was arrested and carried to North Carolina for trial. Soon afterward, the government of Franklin collapsed, and North Carolina passed an act of "pardon and oblivion," and reassumed her government of these people.

The state of Franklin, in 1787–8, was composed of the three original counties of Washington, Sullivan and Greene, together with four new counties—Sevier, which covered the same territory it now covers and a part of what is now Blount; Caswell, which occupied the same section of country now included in Jefferson; Spencer, which covered Hawkins; and Wayne, covering Johnson and Carter.

As late as February, 1789, the record in Jonesboro shows the following entries:

James Allison and James Sevier came into open court and prayed to be admitted to take the benefit of the act of pardon and oblivion by taking the oath provided by law, which was deferred till tomorrow for want of the acts of the General Assembly.

On the next day the following entry was made:

James Sevier, James Allison and Francis Baker, persons *who had withdrawn their allegiance* [from North Carolina] came into open court, and availed themselves of the act of pardon and oblivion by taking the oaths prescribed by law.

At the February term, 1788, of the court, the following order was made and entered of record:

Ordered by the Court that Johnathan Pugh Esqr, Sheriff of Washington County, Take into custody the County court docket of said county, supposed to be in the possession of John Sevier Esqr, And the same records bring from him or any other person or persons, in whose possession they are now, or hereafter shall be, and the same return to the Court or some succeeding court for said county.

At the May term, 1788, this order was made:

Ordered by the court that the Sheriff of this County demand the public records of this County from John Sevier, former clerk of the court.

The records referred to were lost, or remained in the cave where they were hidden.

All opposition to North Carolina authority was now virtually withdrawn, but the people west of the Alleghanies worked quietly for a separation and a new state.

North Carolina passed a second cession act, under the provisions of which, February 25, 1790, Samuel Johnston and Benjamin Hawkins, Senators in Congress from North Carolina, deeded the territory to the United States, and the sovereignty of North Carolina over it instantly expired. It has been aptly said that ''the separation was not like that of a disconsolate mother parting from a beloved daughter, but rather like that when Abraham said to Lot, 'Separate thyself, I pray thee, from me. If thou wilt take the left hand, then I will go to the right; or if thou depart to the right hand, then I will go to the left.'''

President Washington appointed William Blount Governor of the territory, August 7, 1790. On the 10th day of the following October, Governor Blount organized the territorial government, at the house of Mr. Cobb, in Sullivan county, on the north side of Watauga river, since known as the Massengale farm, above and opposite where Austin Springs are. The population of the territory in July, 1791, was 36,043, including 3,417 slaves. The whole population of the Cumberland settlement at that time was 7,042.

November 5, 1791, the second printing press introduced in the ''New World west of the Alleghanies'' was set up, at Rogersville, by Mr. George Roulstone.

The people who made it possible for Tennessee to have a centennial were a wonderful people. Within a period of about fifteen years, they were engaged in three revolutions; participated in organizing and lived under five different governments; established and administered the first free and independent government in America; founded the first church and the first college in the southwest; put in operation the second newspaper in the "New World west of the Alleghanies;" met and fought the British in half a dozen battles, from King's Mountain to the gates of Charleston, gaining a victory in every battle; held in check, beat back and finally expelled from the country four of the most powerful tribes of Indian warriors in America; and left Tennesseans their fame as a heritage, and a commonwealth of which it is their privilege to be proud.

These are the people among whom Andrew Jackson settled and began life, and from whose character, example and achievements he must have received some little degree of inspiration.

Passing from the scene of their toil and trials, their struggles and dangers, from war with the savage and war with the civilized, let us devote a little time to further examination into their character, as revealed in the judicial records made and left by them.

CHAPTER III.

THERE may be mistake, error, fraud and injustice in court proceedings and judicial records; but when such records were made more than a century ago, and contain some part of the history of the people who made them, and have stood all these years unchallenged and uncontradicted, such records may be safely accepted as truth. In writing of a people more than a century after the period in which they lived—a people who did not have a daily newspaper in their midst to chronicle their deeds and views, and who were in a country between which and other parts of the world there was but little if any communication—it is easy indeed for a facile writer to ascribe to them characters which they did not have, views which they did not entertain, and accomplishments with which they were not entitled to be credited, without taking much risk of being contradicted.

The early history of the colonies and "new settlements" in North America is and has been for many years a fascinating field for writers; and it must be confessed that too often a little incident or tradition has been so magnified by a too vivid imagination that it has appeared in print as a very readable but colossal falsehood. It is also lamentable that the plain, unvarnished truth of history has, in many instances, been so colored and distorted in the effort to make it romantic, that many persons who could have contributed much valuable information in the way of simple facts have not done so, because of a lack of that faculty of imagination which some writers possess to such a degree that they can inform you beforehand that they are going to tell you a lie—in part, at least—and yet will tell it in such beautiful language and in so smooth and plausible a way as to make you believe the whole story.

The Tennessee pioneers did not have any one with them in their earliest days to write an account of their experiences, or to portray their lives and characters; nor did they have any newspapers to make a record of their doings in the business concerns and affairs of life; and if they wrote any letters on these matters, they have not been preserved. They had, however, at Jonesboro, a "County Court of Pleas and Quarter Sessions," in which they made and left a record showing much that they did, and from which, even at this late day, we can get a very clear insight into their views as to the duties and responsibilities of citizenship, the power and duty of courts, as well as their notions concerning the business and social relations of life, and indeed on all matters which, in their judgment, pertained in any way to the peace, good fame and welfare of the community and of individuals. I shall, therefore, quote literally much from these old original records kept in Washington county—the quotations being taken from the records of that county only, for the reason that it was the first county established and organized in what is now Tennessee, and included for quite a time all of the early settlements in what is commonly known as "upper East Tennessee." The same character of entries will no doubt be found in the old records kept in Sullivan, Greene, Davidson, Hawkins, Sumner, Tennessee and Knox counties, in all of which Jackson practised as an attorney or presided as a judge. The proceedings in the courts of the counties named, especially those that will be set out, will be of interest not alone to Tennesseans, but also to the descendants, scattered throughout the southwest and west, of the men who made these records.

The first session of the court was held at the log-cabin of Charles Roberson, near Jonesboro, February 23, 1778.   It was composed of the justices of the peace whose names have been given as subscribers to the oath set out in a preceding chapter. After the court had been organized by electing officers, its first act was to fine John Sevier, Jr., for some minor matter which was gravely denominated ''a contempt to the court.''   John Sevier, Sr., had just been elected clerk of the court, and was undoubtedly the most influential man in the country, on account of his meritorious character—but this did not shield the son. The fine was not remitted; and there is no evidence that John Sevier the clerk endeavored in any way to interpose.

On the second day, '' William Cocke by his counsel Waight-sell Avery moved to be admitted to the office of Clerk of this County of Washington which motion was rejected by the Court knowing that John Sevier was entitled to the office.''   This is absolutely the whole of the record.   It was the first contested election case that occurred west of the Alleghany mountains, and was between two citizens who became very distinguished— Cocke having been elected one of the first two Senators from Tennessee, while Sevier, after holding all the other offices within the gift of the people of that county, was elected a representative in Congress and six times chosen Governor of Tennessee. The worthy justices, '' knowing,'' as they said, that Sevier had been elected, without hearing Mr. Cocke, his counsel or any evidence whatsoever, swore in Sevier as clerk.

These entries follow:

Ordered that David Hinkley be fined 30 L. for insulting the Court.

Ordered that Hump Gibson be fined 10 L. for swearing in Court.

Then, after passing upon a motion or two—

Ordered that Ephriam Dunlap Atty. be fined 5 Dollars for insulting the Court, especially Richard White.

It is not likely that any member of this court had ever held any office prior to his appointment as a justice of the peace therein, and it is not probable that many of them had ever been in a court of any kind before they organized that which they constituted; and yet the record shows that, from the first day of the first term, and on through all of the many stormy sessions which they held thereafter, they guarded and defended jealously the dignity of their court, and enforced obedience to its mandates. It was a heinous offence indeed, and visited with condign punishment, to "insult the Court."

The aggregate fines imposed on Sam Tate, at one term, amounted to forty thousand pounds;* and while fines were imposed on some one at every term, there are but two entries to be found on the record, from the February term, 1778, to and including the November term, 1790, showing that such fines were remitted.

At the May term, 1778, a somewhat embarrassing question presented itself. Some one of three persons, it would appear, had taken from Samuel Sherrill,† without his consent, his bay gelding, and left the country. They could not, therefore, get any one of the suspected persons into court or in custody, and they must have been in doubt as to which of the three did in fact ride the horse off; so they said:

On motion it appears that Joshua Williams Johnathan Helms and a certain James Lindley did Feloniously Steal a certain Bay gelding horse from Saml Sherill Senr. Ordered that if the said Saml Sherill can find any property of the said Joshua Williams Johnathan Helms & said Lindley that he take same into his possession.

* Continental currency.

† This was the father of Catherine Sherrill, the "Bonnie Kate" of John Sevier.

So far as the record shows, they never caught any of the defendants, but Sherrill must have got close on them at one time;
for, at the August term, the court "ordered that a saddle and
coat the property of Joshua Williams be sold and the money
arising therefrom be left in the possession of Saml Sherill."
They could not capture and punish the thieves, but they could
and did authorize Sherrill to seize the property of the rascals
wherever he could find it.

The first case of high treason tried by the court was at the
August term, 1778. This is the record:

STATE
        v.   } *High Treason.*
MOSES CRAWFORD.

It is the Opinion of the Court that the defendant be imprisoned during the present war with Great Britain, and the
Sheriff take the whole of his estate into custody which must be
valued by a jury at the next Court and that the one half of the
said estate be kept by the said Sheriff for the use of the State
and the other half remitted to the family of defendant.

I have not examined the statute under which this *county
court* tried, convicted and imprisoned defendants charged with
treason, and confiscated their property, to see whether or not
they had a right to remit one half of confiscated property to the
family of the defendant, for the reason that I do not wish to
know how the fact was.   I am satisified with the record as they
made it, and leave others to look up the statute.

Having disposed of Crawford—and his property too—they
took up the case of Isaac Buller, whom, as he had neither
family nor property, and the evidence, if any was heard (on
motion), was a little vague, they simply put in prison until an
opportunity should offer to make a better use of him.   This is
the summary manner in which they disposed of Isaac:

On motion of Ephriam Dunlap that Isaac Buller Should Be
sent to the Contl. Army, and there to Serve three Years or

During the War On Hearing the facts it is Ordered by the Court That the said Isaac Buller Be Immediately Committed to Gaol and there Safely kept until the said Isaac can be delivered unto A Continent'l Officer to be Conveyed to Head Quarters.

At the February term, 1779, the court made and entered of record an order prescribing the charges that tavern-keepers might exact from guests as follows:

Diet 08s.0: Lodging 1 night good bed and clean sheets 1s. 6d: Rum Wine or Brandy 3L.4s.0: Toddy pr Quart, & sprts of Rum therein 8s.0. and so in proportion. Corn or Oats per Gal 4s.0: Stabledge with hay or fodder 24 hrs 4s. 0: Pasturage 24 hrs. 2s: Cyder pr qrt 4s.0: Bear pr qrt 2s.0: Whisky pr Gallon 2L.0.0:

After they had put the above on record, they entered upon the trial of their second case of a very high crime, as the following entry shows:

STATE
vs.   *For Treason Feby 1779*
GEORGE LEIVIS.

On hearing the facts and considering the testimony of the Witnesses It is the Opinion of the Court That the defendant be sent to the District Gaol It Apg. To the Court that the said Leivis is a spie or An Officer from Florida out of the English Army.

At this term, besides transacting routine business, they tried ten persons on charges of treason, convicted five of them, ordered their property confiscated, and sent them to the district jail at Salisbury—and the entire record of the term is contained on twelve pages!

If this court could have been transferred to the more intelligent states of Massachusetts or New Hampshire, and had held a few terms therein, ''Shays's rebellion'' would have been crushed out in a week, or all the ''gaols'' would have been filled with the rebellious and the public treasury with the proceeds of confiscated property. These patriots were in earnest.

At the May term, 1779, two entries appear as having been made on the same day, which show two sides of this remarkable court. The first entry is as follows:

STATE
v.
PAT MURPHEY } *For stealing a Ploughshear, hogs and some other Things*

The Court are of Opinion that the defendant pay 33L. 6s. 8d. to Zachr. Isbell for his Hog & 26L. 13s. 4 to Thos. Evans for his Hog and ten pounds fine And also receive Twenty Lashes on his bare Back well laid on by the Sheriff or Deputy.

The other entry was:

Ordered that John Murphey be fined the sum of Twenty pounds for Ill Treatment to his reputed father Pat Murphey.

The court said that, in its opinion, Pat Murphey was a bad man—and he was, as other cases in the records against him show; and they had him whipped, fined him and, under the operation of the court's adjustable jurisdiction, rendered judgment against him in a criminal case for the value of two hogs; but these "backwoods" justices of the peace said to the reputed son of this old and hardened criminal that "Ill Treatment" of a father, by even a reputed son, would not be tolerated in that community.

At this May term, and following the entries just given, is another, which, in a few words and (so far as the record shows) without any previous notice, deprives a citizen of his liberty and of further opportunity to do harm to "the common cause of liberty," on the mere motion of the state's attorney. Here it is:

On motion of E. Dunlap State Attorney it is ordered that John Holly for his Ill practices in Harboring and Abetting disorderly persons who are prejudicial and Inimical to the Common Cause of Liberty and Frequently Disturbing our public Tranquility in Genl. be Imprisoned for the Term & Time of One Year.

Up to the date of the entry of this order imprisoning John Holly "for the term and time of one year," on the mere motion of the state's attorney, the record shows a little more formality in convictions for treason and the confiscation of property, as it will appear from the recitals that the court, "on considering the facts," or "on hearing the witnesses [or evidence]," "are of opinion," etc.

It is very doubtful whether there can be found (outside of Tennessee) another such judicial record as this one, made and entered on a mere motion, without the accused having previous notice or (so far as the record shows) being present in person or by attorney, and without any evidence being heard to support the charge, embodied in the motion, that Holly was an enemy to the public tranquillity generally and guilty of other specified offences. It is safe to assume, however, that the court "knew" he was guilty, as they "knew" that John Sevier was entitled to the office of clerk when they dismissed Cocke's contest without hearing him at all.

At this term, the court "nominated and appointed John Sevier, Jesse Walton and Zachr. Isbell to take into possession such property as should be confiscated," and they gave "bond as such commissioners in the sum of Five Hundred and Fifty Thousand pounds."

And they had the "tax-dodger" with them also, as early as August, 1779—the good citizen who always wants his full share of attention and protection by the law, without paying his just proportion of the taxes to support the government; but he could not escape this court's resourceful remedies for all exigencies. Here is given the disposition of the case:

Ordered that the Sheriff Collect from Wm. More four fold: his Taxable property being apraised by the Best Information that John Woods, Jacob Brown & Johnathan Tipton Assessors could get—to the sum of Eight thousand pounds.

Even the smart and rascally tax-dodger could not evade the law, with a court like that one to take hold of him.

At the May term, 1780, it was ``Ord. that a fine of One Hundred pounds be imposed on John Chisholm Esqr for being Guilty of Striking and Beating Abram Denton in the Court Yard also Disturbing the peace and Decorum of the Court and that the Clerk issue an execution for the same.'' This fine is here set out for the reason that John Chisholm was one of the first justices appointed for the county—he was at the time a member of the court that imposed this fine—and, as the records show, was wealthy and prominent in public affairs, being trusted with various appointments by the court; and yet he did not escape the hand of correction so often laid on offenders by the court in one or another way. The offence for which he was fined was committed, not in the presence of the court, but out in the court-yard. I very much doubt if an instance prior to this one can be found, where the limits within which it has been held that a contempt of court could be committed have been so extended as to include the court-yard.

At the November term, 1780, the court formulated and entered the following very remarkable order:

The Court appointed John Sevier, William Cobb, Thomas Houghton and Andrew Greer Commissioners for the County to be Judges of the Different kinds of paper Emissions in Circulation in this County or may be hereafter, in order to prevent frauds and Impositions that might be committed on said County, and for the purpose of Detecting and Suppressing Coins of this kind, who shall be the Judges & Viewers of all such Monies.

The record recites that these commissioners and judges ``took the oath and entered into bond for the performance of sd Trust.''

. At the time these four gentlemen were appointed as a high commission to be ``judges and viewers'' of the currency of the realm, and ``detectors and suppressers'' of spurious or counterfeit "coins" and "paper emissions in circulation," all kinds of "such monies" seem to have gotten into "the new world west of the Alleghanies," for, at the same term of the court making the order regulating the charges of tavern-keepers, referred to above, two rates or schedules were prescribed, one in "paper emissions," the other in "coins." The order of the county court creating this commission and investing it with power to "view" and "judge" of the genuineness of the circulating medium, and to detect and suppress such of it as should be adjudged fraudulent, does not point out the way, lay down any rules or provide any method for the guidance and direction of the commission in the exercise of the powers given or the discharge of the duties imposed. It says simply what they shall do, or rather what they have been appointed to do, and then leaves them to do it. That they found out an effective way to exercise their powers there is not a doubt. They did not need to be given "mandatory" power. "Counterfeiters" had been "dealt with," before this domestic monetary commission was created, by some of the same men who constituted the commission.

One of the most delicate and difficult duties that devolved upon this commission, under the terms of the order creating it— particularly the words, "in order to prevent frauds and impositions that might be committed," etc.—was in cases where a question was raised as to the genuineness of the money offered in payment by a citizen known to be upright and free from any suspicion of handling spurious money, to another equally honest, who refused it because he was doubtful as to its being "good money." The "judges and viewers" were called in to take action, and had to decide in effect whether or not the money offered was a "legal tender." Their decision was accepted; and henceforth that particular money circulated, if so ordered, without question, and performed all the functions of money, whether it was in fact genuine or spurious: if the decision was adverse, that money was thenceforth worthless.

As an incident of the power and authority vested in these "judges and viewers," arose the question occasionally of guilt or innocence, when a charge of counterfeiting or of wilfully and knowingly passing spurious money was preferred. The person so charged was tried before the high currency commission, and its finding or judgment not only settled the question of the guilt or innocence of the accused, but made the particular currency involved either "sound money" or counterfeit in that entire country. John Sevier, according to tradition, was chairman of the commission; if his name was written on the "paper emission," it passed current thereafter, and when offered in payment was a "legal tender."

The court also "Ordered that Capt. John Patterson deliver unto John Halley a Certain Rifle Gun being the property of said John Halley."

Some very serious difference or grave misunderstanding between the court and Mr. James Gibson must have occurred at the November term, 1780, or at some time previous, if the record left in reference thereto be correct—and who would doubt it? Whether or not the court intended to suppress freedom of speech generally, it must be admitted that its action toward Gibson would certainly tend toward suppressing the public expression of a want of confidence in the integrity of that court, and putting a stop to the practice of "throwing out speeches" against it. The record relates that—

James Gibson being brought before the Court, for throughing Out Speeches Against the Court, to-wit,—Saying that the Court was purjured and would not do Justice, and Other Glareing Insults. The Court On Considering the matter are of Opinion that the said James Gibson is guilty of a flagrant

Breach of The peace & for the same and the glareing and Dare-
ing insults offered to the Court do order that the said James
Gibson be fined the sum of fifteen thousand pounds & that he
be kept in custody until same is secured.

Gibson, as the record shows, secured the fine. It is not to
be supposed that any of the "speeches" which he had been
"throwing out" were made in the court room or in hearing of
the court, because the record states that he was "brought before the court." When and where he assailed this august body
does not appear. This did not matter to them: their jurisdiction was as wide as the universe, and their power to punish
him unquestionable, as they believed. The fine imposed on
John Chisholm, a member of the court, for striking and beating Abram Denton out in the court-yard; the fine imposed on
John Murphey, for "ill treatment" of his reputed father, no
doubt at home; the order directing Capt. Patterson to deliver
"unto John Halley" a gun decided by the court to be "the
property of said John Halley"; the method employed to punish Gibson; the creation of a commission to determine in effect
what money should or should not be a legal tender, as well as
the other matters, hereafter to be related, to which they gave
attention, show that this remarkable court had no idea of having its powers limited and defined or its jurisdiction circum-
scribed.

Only two orders of the May term, 1781, will be noticed.
The first is, "Ord, that Saml Tate be fined the sum of ten
thousand pounds* for a contempt of Court and that the Clerk
issue F. Facious vs his estate for the same." On a subsequent
day of the term, the clerk acknowledges the receipt of the fine
imposed on Tate. The other order is: "Ordered that Jesse
Greer be fined the sum of One Hundred pounds for a Contempt

* It must constantly be kept in mind that these apparently enormous sums were
in Continental currency.

4

offered to the Court &c in refusing to deliver unto the Widow
Dyckes her property as Directed By Order of the Court."
Under *their* rules of practice, they did not require "the Widow
Dyckes" to employ a lawyer and bring an action of replevin
against Greer; they had heard the case at a former term "on
motion," without stating on the record who made the motion,
and had directed Greer to deliver the property in question to
the widow Dyckes, which he had refused to do.   They did not
require her to employ counsel to sue Greer and recover a judgment for the value of the property detained from her, issue
execution, levy on and sell the property to satisfy the judgment; they made use of a much more direct method, by holding Mr. Greer liable for contempt, and resorting to their favorite mode of administering justice without delay—to-wit, "on
motion" and "ordered."

At the May term, 1782, nothing of any considerable consequence was done.   The court "nominated and appointed John
Sevier William Cocke and Valentine Sevier Commissioners of
Confiscation for the year 1782, whereupon sd. Comr's entered
into bond with security for the sum of Fifteen Thousand
pounds, Specie."

The court, at this term, gave to a citizen who had evidently
been "hiding out" permission to return to the settlements, as
the following order shows:

On motion that Joshua Baulding should be admitted to come
in and Remain henceforth peaceably in this County.   On pro-
viso, that he comply with the Laws provided for persons being
inimical to the State and have Rendered Service that will ex-
piate any Crime that he has been Guilty of inimical to this
State or the United States.   The Court on considering the same
Grant the sd Leave.

This order, and others similar to it, which are not given place
in this chapter, serve to establish beyond question the intense

loyalty of the members of the court to "the common cause of liberty" (as the struggle of the Americans then going on against Great Britain was always designated), and also the vigilance with which they must have scrutinized the conduct of each individual. There can be no doubt that Baulding had fled and was hiding in the hills or mountains, and that he knew it would not be safe to return or "come in" without the permission of the court.

The August term, 1782, was one of the most memorable in the history of the court. It was a "Court of Oyer and Terminer & Genl. Gaol Delivery," as well as for other county purposes. At this term it was presided over for the first time by a judge—"the Honl. Spruce McCay Esqr Present and Presiding." He had the court opened by proclamation, and with all the formality and solemnity characterizing the opening of the English courts.

On the first day of the term, John Vann was found guilty, by a jury, of horse-stealing, the punishment for which at that time was death. On the same day the record contains an entry to the effect that "the Jury who passed upon the Tryal of John Vann beg Leave to Recommend him to the Court for Mercy"; but no mercy was shown him by "the Honl. Spruce McCay Esqr," as the record discloses further along. During the week, two more unfortunates—Isaac Chote and William White—were found guilty of horse-stealing; and, on the last day of the term (August 20), Judge McCay disposes of all three of these criminals in one order, as follows: "Ord that John Vann Isaac Chote & Wm White now Under Sentence of Death be executed on the tenth day of September next." This is the whole of the entry.

The judge was mistaken in saying that the three persons named in the order were "under sentence of death." No such sentence is to be found of record—all that appears is an entry of the style of the case, as "State vs " etc., in each case, and the entry opposite the case, that "the jury sworn to pass upon the Tryal do find the defendant guilty in manner and form as charged in the indictment"; but there is no formal sentence of death entered of record in either of the three cases. It is not probable that a parallel proceeding can be found in judicial history.   Judge McCay utterly ignored the unanimous action of the jury who recommended John Vann to the mercy of the court. Can a case be found where a judge, in the United States, ever refused mercy to a criminal who was commended to him for mercy by the jury that found him guilty ?   Can another case be found where a judge caused three persons to be "executed " by one order, consisting of five lines and seventeen words, exclusive of the names of the criminals ?

Judge McCay omits entirely to direct the method of executing the three criminals—he does not say whether they shall be hanged, shot, burned or drowned—but they were executed, either with rope, rifle or tomahawk, according to the good taste of the sheriff or the wishes of the defendants.

Tradition in that country gave Judge McCay the character of a heartless tyrant. He was said, while judge, to have always been on one side or the other of suits tried before him; and he never failed to let it be known which side he was on. He frequently indulged in lecturing, not to say abusing, juries publicly, when they returned verdicts contrary to his wishes and instructions.   But "the Honl. Spruce McCay Esqr" found his match in the juries. They could not be driven or intimidated into giving verdicts contrary to their convictions; and whenever they differed with the judge—and they always knew his views—in a case of weight or serious results, they would deliberately disperse, go to their homes, and not return any more during that term of court. In a case styled "State vs Taylor," the record shows that the jury was sworn and the defendant put on "Tryal." Nothing more appears except the following significant entry: "State vs. Taylor. The jury having failed to come back into court, it is therefore a mistrial."

Judge McCay may only have been, as has been said of him, "a man of strong character, determined and fearless in discharging his duty"—but so were the juries in that county, as the records show.

At the May term, 1783, there was made an entry, which, when taken in connection with one which will be given immediately after it, will show how wisely these pioneers judged of men, and how necessary, sometimes, it was for them to take measures which at the time appeared harsh and cruel. The first entry is as follows:

On petition of Lewis & Elias Pybourn that they who is at this time Lying out and keep themselves Secreted from Justice that the Court would permit them to Return to their Respective Houses and places of abode and Them the said Lewis & Elias Pybourn to give bond and sufficient Security for their Good behavior &c. The Court on consideration of the matter do Grant and Give Leave unto said Elias & Lewis Pybourn to Return accordingly on their giving bond & approved security to Capt. John Newman for their Good behavior &c.

A final entry, made in the "Superior Court of Law and Equity" at Jonesboro, seven years later—at the August term, 1790—in the case of the "State of North Carolina Against Elias Pybourn for Horse Stealing," justifies the members of the Court of Pleas and Quarter Sessions in having required Elias Pybourn to give security for his future good behavior. The full entry is as follows:

The defendant being called to the Bar and asked if he had anything to say why sentence should not be passed upon him Saith Nothing. It is therefore Ordered that the said Elias

Pybourn be confined in the publick Pillory one Hour.   That he
have both his ears nailed to the Pillory and severed from his
Head; That he receive at the publick Whipping post thirty nine
lashes well laid On; and be branded on the Right cheek with
the letter H, and on his left cheek with the letter T. and that
the Sheriff of Washington County put this sentence in execution between the hours of Twelve and Two this day.

Horrible, awful punishment!   Marked for life; a description
of his crime burned on and into his face with a hot iron—
"Horse Thief"; both of his ears cut off close up to his head.
What a hideous spectacle!   Was the mark placed upon Cain by
the Almighty such that when people met him they said, "Let
him alone; keep your hands off him; he has been punished
sufficiently already"?   Would not people say the same of poor,
debased, degraded Pybourn?

Was the punishment inflicted on Pybourn barbarous?   Yes;
but the court had warned him of the wrath to come, and had
first made him flee to the forest for safety—better had he gone
to the Indians—and had then given him permission to return
to his home, on condition that he would reform and behave
himself.   The only entry found in the whole of the records to
soften in the slightest degree the harsh and (it may be said) inhuman punishment meted out to Pybourn, is one that suggests
the horror that came over one Joseph Culton, when he discovered, after he had emerged from a single combat with Charles
Young, that the latter had bitten off one of his ears.   Culton
of course regretted the loss of his ear, and was still more an-
noyed to be thus disfigured for life; but these were the least of
his troubles—somebody thereafter might think that he had
been "cropped" for crime.   What was he to do?   He appeared
at the November term, 1788, of the Court of Pleas and Quarter
Sessions, whose jurisdiction knew no limits as to venue, time
when or subject matter, and the following entry was made for
his relief and protection from suspicion:

Joseph Culton comes into Court and Proved by Oath of Alexander Moffit that he lost a part of his left Ear in a fight with a certain Charles Young and prays the same to be entered of record. Ordered therefore that the same be Admitted Accordingly.

It is not probable that any one ever examined this entry, and demanded to see the page whereon the lost ear had been formally entered of record; but it is certain that Joseph Culton carried with him constantly a certified copy of the entry which attested that he had been maimed in honorable combat, and not as a punishment for violation of law.

This wonderful county court, before and since which there has been none like it, adapted or adjusted its jurisdictional powers and methods to all matters, questions and conditions that could be brought in any way to its notice. When a stranger came into the community, it did not content itself with letting him alone, no matter how quietly and orderly he might conduct himself; it had him interviewed, as the entry here quoted will prove:

The Court Order that Wm Clary a trancient person give security for his behavior, and return to his family within five months, as the said Clary is without any pass or recommendation and confesses he left his family and have taken up with another woman.

The most that the average detective could have gotten out of Clary would have been that he came from—where he started, and was going—where he went; but the court found out more than this about him, and they must have got it from his own mouth, as the order, after reciting facts that they could have gotten from him only, concludes by setting forth a very damaging confession which he had made, and which, all will agree, justified the court in requiring security of him for his behavior while he might remain in their midst, and peremptorily ordering him to return to his family within a stated time.

By the time of the meeting of the August term, 1784, the court had pretty well purged the country of traitors, horse thieves, "trancients," etc. At this term the court seems to have turned its attention to the ugly habits of some of the very respectable; for, on the first day of the term, as the record shows, fines were imposed and paid as follows: " Eml. Carter three prophane oaths 8s. 10d. pd: Pharoh Cobb four prophane oaths 10s. 8d. pd: Buckner Nantz One prophane swearing Oath prays mercy Granted: Valentine Sevier for prophanely swearing 4 Oaths fined 10s. 8d. pd: Mark Mitchell for swearing One prophane Oath fined 2s. 8d. Patrick Murphey One Oath, Michael Tylloy Two Oaths." This treatment seems to have been effective; for, no fines being recorded after the first day, it is reasonably sure that no "prophane oaths" were indulged in, during the remainder of the term—at least in hearing of the court.

As a result of the many battles with the Indians, and the numerous Indian massacres which had occurred, numbers of children were left without fathers or mothers. They had no orphan asylum, but the records of the court show that homes were provided for these wards, nevertheless, by the Watauga and King's Mountain heroes. They had no county asylum for the poor; but the county court, whose jurisdiction could be extended to meet all emergencies, "ordered" some citizen by name to "take and keep" the person named therein for the time specified. These orders contained no recital that they were made by the consent of anyone—they emanated from the inherent power and duty of the court, as it believed, to provide for the poor.

The entries and orders selected from these old records are given, in order that those who wish to know something of the views, characters and abilities of the very earliest pioneers of

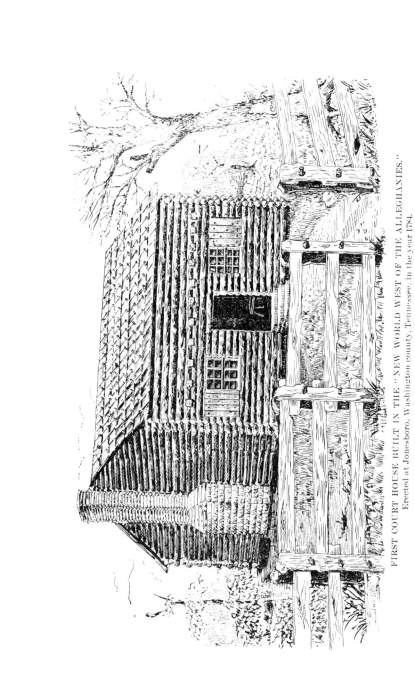

FIRST COURT HOUSE BUILT IN THE "NEW WORLD WEST OF THE ALLEGHANIES."

Erected at Jonesboro, Washington county, Tennessee, in the year 1784.

Tennessee, may read for themselves the views and opinions which they placed in solemn form on court records, in reference to the various matters, questions and conditions on which, as they thought, the vicissitudes of the times made it necessary for them to take action. I wish to give, at this place, two more orders of the court, before closing this chapter. At the November term, 1784, the following was entered on the record:

The Court recommend that there be a Court House built in the following manner, to wit: 24 feet square diamond corners and hewed down after the same is built up, 9 feet high between the two floors, and the body of the house 4 feet high above the upper floor, each floor to be neatly laid with plank. The roof to be of joint shingles neatly hung on with pegs, a Justices bench, A lawyers and a Clerks bar, also a Sheriffs box to sit in.

At the November term, 1785, the following was entered:

The Court Ordered that Col'o Charles Roberson be allowed fifty pounds Current money for the building of the Court House in the Town of Jones Borough.

As this was the first court house erected in what is now Tennessee, and the one in which Andrew Jackson, John McNairy, Archibald Roane, William Cocke, David Campbell and others began their professional careers; and in and about which John Sevier, though not a lawyer, rendered so much and such invaluable service in laying the foundations of our state, and its civil as well as military institutions, I have had.it reproduced, and present a picture of it in this little volume. From what has been said, and from the records which have been quoted, the imagination can picture the scenes and proceedings occurring in this "temple of justice"—for such it was, although made of logs "hewed down" and covering "hung on with pegs."

These early records challenge comparison, in spirit, form and substance, with any others made during the same period in any community, country or state in the United States. No patriotic, intelligent people can read them without being filled with admiration and inspired with respect and reverence for the men who made them. They said, on the first day of the first term of the court, the court must be respected; to the cruel son, you shall not ill-treat your father, though he be a criminal; to the vagrant without a "pass or recommendation," you must give security for your behavior or leave the community; to the man who had abandoned his wife, you must return to your family; to the strong and influential, you must render unto the widow her own, or we will force you to do so by fines that will make you glad to obey; to the tax-dodger, you shall pay your proportion of the taxes; to a member of the court, no matter what your position is, if you cruelly beat your neighbor, we will take from you a large part of your wealth and turn it into the public treasury; to the man who was "throwing out speeches" calculated to destroy the influence of the court for good, you must not malign the court, no matter when nor where—if you do, we will lay the heavy hand of summary punishment upon you; to such as were stirring up sedition and opposition to "the common cause of liberty," you shall not remain openly and peaceably in the community without giving security for your good conduct; to thieves, we will fine, whip, brand and hang you; to tories, we will confiscate your property and imprison you; to the British, we will meet and fight you, on every field from the mountains to the sea; to the Indians, we will fight you too, from the mountains to the lakes and the gulf. And they did it all. Who could have done more? They were heroes, one and all, but history, it seems, has long since given them over to oblivion.

Although, in 1788, they had passed through a "general insurrection of the times," as chronicled by the clerk of the court under the state of Franklin, and had no doubt come out somewhat demoralized, still the habit of doing what they believed to be right was so strongly imbedded in their natures that, at a term of court (February, 1788) held after its reorganization following the Franklin collapse, they imposed upon and collected from one of the most prominent citizens of the county a fine for swearing in the court-yard. The record recites that "Leroy Taylor came into Court and pays into the Office the fine prescribed by Acts of Assembly for one profane Oath which was accepted of. Ordered therefore that he be discharged. 21s." Leroy Taylor was elected from Washington county as a delegate to the constitutional convention of 1796, and was kept in the General Assembly almost continuously for eight or ten sessions after Tennessee was admitted into the Union; he was the author and introducer of the first resolution offered in the General Assembly (in 1801), raising a committee to prepare a design for the great seal of the state of Tennessee—but, with all his prominence, he could not with impunity make use of even "one profane oath" in hearing of the county court of Washington county.

The achievements of these old pioneers will run, however, "like the covenants of warranty with the land" they loved so well. A few glimmering memories, a few dim traditions, some scattered fragments of stories—these are all that is left (outside the old court records alluded to) of many of these men, every one of whom was a giant in morals and a colossus in intellect, as compared with many modern pigmies whose little deeds have been magnified into great achievements.

If the structures of state, county and municipal institutions in Tennessee, and the social fabric as well, had been kept in harmony with the pure, simple, steadfast and enduring foundations laid by John Sevier and his contemporaries, what models we would have today for the world to imitate. Are we wiser or better than they? Read and study these old records: then answer.

CHAPTER IV.

A TRAGIC EPISODE.

TENNESSEE does not need the prolific genius of the romanticist to embellish and invest with thrilling interest the narrative of her origin and development, of the hardships and endurance of her pioneers, of the heroism and triumphs of her builders and defenders; but, looking backward, with more than a century between us and the Revolutionary War, we would be unmanly not to admit that at times we were a little too vindictive and remorseless in pursuing those whose reverence 'and love for the "mother country" were stronger than their desire for a change and greater than their faith in the young dream of American liberty.

Whilst separation and independence were imposing theories, so fascinating to the wild and restless spirits who had founded and were building up a vast empire in the western world, advocating their bold measures with absorbing zeal and desperate earnestness, there was a minority, many of whom were staid and sturdy, honest in purpose and courageous in conviction, who regarded the movement as unwarranted, and fraught with immediate peril and ultimate ruin. Despite persuasion, remonstrance, threats, social ostracism and what seemed to them persecution, they held allegiance to the Crown as a paramount duty, and regarded the war that must inevitably follow, in its destruction of the flower of the new country, as a twin horror of the Cretan Minotaur that fed on the Athenian youth.

At the close of the Revolutionary War, these tories ("loyalists," as they called themselves) were universally execrated;

and the most popular victor, with many of the patriots, was he who could suggest the most humiliating punishment for these unfortunates: they were put in stocks, chained to the public pillories, cast into prison, and beggared by the confiscation of their property, "without benefit of clergy." These and other punishments inflicted on the tories were justified during the times as retaliatory for outrages committed upon the patriots by the British and some of their American allies. Then, too, some extenuation must be found for the victorious revolutionists in the riot of frenzy and demoralization that always follows war.*

In the perspective of this group of terrible scenes, heartaches, desolation of homes and disruption of families that the "common cause of liberty" might not perish, stands out a tragedy which, while it is of itself a melancholy picture of misfortune, suffering, despair and absolute want, is yet luminous with courageous manhood and the transcendent glory and conquering heroism of a pure and noble womanhood.

Novr Term 1780. Ordered that the Commissioners advertise and sell the property of James Crawford & Thomas Barker, they the said James Crawford and Thomas Barker being found and taken in Arms Against the State.

May Term 1782: John Sevier a Commissioner of Confiscated property for the year 1781, made return that he sold Two Slaves Confiscated of the estate of Thomas Barker at the price of thirty four Hundred pounds, and that he have the money ready to Return.

Aug. Term 1782. The Court Order that Mrs. Ann Barker wife of Thomas Barker who stands charged with joining the British & was taken at Kings Mountain a prisoner, by the Americans & after that his estate was Confiscated by the County Court of Washington—On her application in behalf of her Husband for Tryal by Jury the same is Accordingly Granted.

---

* If the motives that prompted many of the tories to adhere to the British crown during the Revolution were measured by the more modern political standards of selfishness or self-interest, there be many now who could not make mouths at their memories.

These musty old records kept at Jonesboro, stitched together like an old-fashioned copy-book, unbound, "unhonored and unsung," have slumbered for more than a century. They contain history so sacred, however, that not a mouse or a moth has dared to touch them; the paper is still good and the ink and penmanship clear and legible; and, if properly cared for, they will be as enduring almost as the principles of justice and integrity that guided the men who made them.

Connected with, growing out of and clustering around some entries and orders in these almost forgotten archives of a bygone century, there are stories and traditions which, if they could be unravelled, touched up and then put together again by a skilful and painstaking historian, would thrill with awe, admiration and wonder many of the present generation, and arouse in them sentiments and sympathies far more ennobling and exalting than those aroused by the ephemeral literature of the day. One only of these stories and traditions have I been able to trace and treasure up, for the purpose of giving it to the public at such time as I should think proper.

I have grouped the three entries given above, for the purpose of publishing (for the first time, so far as I know) one of the saddest and most pathetic of the many sad and pathetic stories of the times. The mere reading of these three short entries suggests not only to Tennesseans, but to Americans, a whole history: the Revolutionary War, King's Mountain, treason, confiscation, imprisonment, wife and children reduced to want, the faithfulness of the wife and her final appeal in person to the court for a trial of her husband by jury. But these entries have their own peculiar and painful history, which will be related briefly, as obtained from sources which would make doubt, on my part at least, undutiful and discrediting to my ancestors.

Thomas Barker came to the Watauga country immediately preceding or just after the formal Declaration of Independence was made by the colonies. He came from either southeastern Virginia or Maryland. He was a large, handsome man, over the average in intelligence. He brought with him a fair library for the times, the best of household and kitchen furniture, some slaves and plenty of live stock and farming utensils. His purpose was to acquire an immense estate in lands, which he was preparing to do when the Revolution broke out in earnest. He was a "tory" from the start, and did not attempt to conceal his views, which were, in brief, that the colonies were too weak to contend successfully with Great Britain; that the latter, with her wealth and facilities, would ultimately crush out all opposition, and the colonies would be reduced in resources and yet subjected to burdens more oppressive than those complained of; or, if they were successful in gaining their independence, they would not be able to agree among themselves upon such form of government as would permanently unite them into one people, offensive and defensive; that no matter what form of government they might adopt for uniting all of the colonies into one whole, they would soon become disaffected and dissolve their relations to each other, thereby becoming a scattered, weak and helpless people for more powerful nations to prey upon and subjugate; and that it was better to yield obedience to and enjoy the protection of the "mother country."

These views had been expressed by Barker to the court which afterward confiscated his property, as early as the February term, 1779, at which term he was arraigned on a charge of "treason." Barker also stated to the court that it was not his desire to take sides in the struggle; that he preferred, if let alone, to remain with them and his wife and children, but that, if forced to participate on one side or the other, he should take up arms for the "mother country." He was a brave man and an honest, and the court knew it; and they disposed of the case—which was styled "State vs Thomas Barker for Treason" —by the following order: "On hearing the facts It is the Opinion of the Court that he the Deft. be discharged." As the war progressed, however, the feeling of hate and bitterness in the community against "tories" became more and more intense, and Barker finally left his home and joined the British army. He was captured at King's Mountain by some of the very men who constituted the court to which he had so boldly expressed his views more than a year before. He had been made a captain, and, according to tradition, commanded a company of tories at the battle. He was not only a man of personal courage, but he was a proud, "high-strung" fellow, about twenty-eight or thirty years old; and, at the moment of the surrender of the remnant of Ferguson's army, he was denouncing in bitter terms the cowardice of his own and other troops.

After the battle of King's Mountain, the Americans from Virginia and from Washington and Sullivan counties, North Carolina, started home with the prisoners, arms, etc., captured in the battle. On the way, about October 12 to 14, a court martial was held at a point called Bickerstaff's Old Field, in Rutherford county, North Carolina, and some thirty or more of the prisoners were sentenced to be hanged—some for desertion from the American army, others for horse-stealing, and still others for crimes and outrages perpetrated on the people who were supporting the "common cause of liberty." None of those so sentenced were regular British soldiers; they were North Carolina tories, some of them from Washington and Sullivan counties. Among the latter were Thomas Barker and James Crawford, who were saved from the ignominious death to which they had been sentenced, and which was actually in-

flicted on nine or ten of the prisoners, by the intervention of
their former friends and neighbors who were then present as
soldiers in the commands of Sevier and Shelby. Barker and
Crawford knew the men who had captured them, and knew
that as a class they were both brave and just. Barker's bearing, during and after the court martial proceedings, was cool
and defiant; he said, with much deliberation, that he was not
guilty of a single one of the offences charged against him, and
that there were more than a hundred men there who knew him
and knew his statement to be true; and he added that, if they
stood by and permitted him to be hanged for crimes he was incapable of committing, then he was no judge of men.

This speech infuriated some, of the men from Washington
and Sullivan counties and Virginia, and they made some demonstrations of instant violence upon the speaker, who stood with
a scowl upon his face, and, holding up his open hands, said
quietly: "I am unarmed; you can kill me, but you can't scare
me!" His speech, however, had quite a different effect upon
those who knew him at home, those who knew his wife, and
especially those who knew him to be a brave, truthful, honest
man. Col. Charles Roberson, John McNab, Charles Allison
and John Allison,* who had participated in the battle of King's
Mountain, interposed with earnestness and emphasis against
hanging Barker and Crawford, and they were supported in
their opposition by Col. John Sevier and Col. Isaac Shelby,
which of course settled it. Barker was brought back to Jonesboro and put in prison, where he had been kept for a little
more than a year and ten months, when his noble wife appeared
in court in person, and procured the order granting him a trial
by jury, given above.

This August term, 1782, was one long talked of and remem-

* Grandfather of the writer.

5

bered for more reasons than one. It was the term at which a judge—"the Honl. Spruce McCay Esqr."—presided for the first time; the term at which three horse-thieves had been tried and sentenced to be executed; the term at which tories had been tried and sentenced to imprisonment, and their property confiscated; the term at which some offenders were sentenced to be, and were, whipped at the public whipping-post.* Few, very few women would have gone in person before such a court, to demand that a tory be granted a trial by jury; but Mrs. Antoinette Barker, wife of Thomas Barker, walked into court, with two (possibly three) small children with her. Their appearance was sufficient to excite sympathy: their faces were pale and haggard, and their clothing, although neat, was patched and worn. Mrs. Barker was a woman of fine appearance, with a beautiful face and a symmetrical figure, and more than a match for the court in intelligence; but, depicted in every line of her countenance, were the traces of mental anguish and physical suffering. She did not, however, weep, go into hysterics, faint, fall down and be carried out, but she stood up in the presence of that court, in all the magnificence of superior womanhood, and, with the vehement eloquence of despair, pleaded the cause of her husband. All that she said will never be known; some things that she said were handed down from generation to generation. She "used the Declaration of Independence on the court"; she denied that her husband was a traitor; she reminded the justices that he had stated his views to them openly and boldly, that he had never taken the oath of allegiance to the continental cause, and that he had told them plainly that, if forced to a choice, he would go into the British army; that he was her husband, and a kind and good one, and the father of her little, innocent, helpless children; that they

* See chapter iii.

had taken all of his property and left his family paupers; that he was then in prison, and had been for nearly two years, in consequence of which his health was altogether gone; that she and her little ones were without a protector, and that her neighbors and former friends had almost wholly forsaken her. Her face, no doubt, was flushed with the hot blood of agony welling up from her heart; possibly her voice grew weak and broke under the stress of her emotion—but this noble woman won her cause. Her application for the trial of her husband by a jury was granted, and the court immediately adjourned. The record shows it, and the adjourning order is signed by Andrew Greer, James Stewart, Charles Roberson, Charles Allison, Thomas Houghton and John McNab, four of whom at least had participated in the capture of Thomas Barker at King's Mountain, and had afterward been present at his trial by court martial.

This heroine, in the wilds of the western world, had undoubtedly quoted from the Declaration of Independence the charge against Great. Britain ''for depriving us in many cases of the benefits of trial by jury,'' and had also probably suggested to the mind of the court, for the first time, the question as to whether treason could be committed against a government by a person who had never acknowledged allegiance to it.

The order granting Barker a trial by jury, unlike other orders of this court, is not clear. It bears on its face evidence of confusion in the court; and this, taken in connection with the fact that the court adjourned immediately after granting the order, renders it certain that this wonderful woman was, for the time being, in absolute control of this marvellous court.

Did she try to secure the services of a lawyer and fail? I do not know; but I do know that these old records fail to disclose the presence of an attorney as counsel for a single one of the various defendants who were tried by the court on a charge of treason. There were at this time, according to the old records, about six attorneys practising regularly in the court, and the records recite their presence as counsel in other cases at that and other courts. Were these attorneys too patriotic to appear in these cases, or too timid from a personal or business standpoint?

The court afterward relented, and Barker was released on his own recognizance, and never tried. Ruined in fortune, ostracized by friends, broken in spirit and in health, he could not endure his changed condition in life. He died soon after his release from prison, and the brave, faithful, noble but broken-hearted wife speedily followed her husband to the grave, leaving two or three children, the oldest a boy of some five or six years. They were taken by a gentleman and his wife who had no children, but a brother of either Barker or his wife soon came and removed them from scenes and faces that it was well for them to forget forever.

The little graveyard in which this brave man and his noble wife were buried was remembered by old people in Washington and Sullivan counties as late as thirty years ago. When I first saw and knew this graveyard as the one in which they were buried, it looked much like a thicket fenced in, but the old crooked rail fence around it was fast rotting down. There were some large trees in it, the largest a wild cherry. Later, the fence was entirely gone, as well as most of the trees, and cattle were lying on the graves in the shade of the trees. Still later, the trees were all gone save the lone wild cherry, and there was not a stone or a mound left: the owner of the land was plowing over the dust of the dead.

The world's heroes are not those only who talk face to face with death at the cannon's mouth, and wet battle-fields with their crimson life-tide.

CHAPTER V.

THE first legislative act passed in what is now the state of Tennessee was an "Ordinance of the Governor and Judges of the Territory of the United States of America South of the River Ohio, for circumscribing the counties of Greene and Hawkins, and laying out two new counties, Jefferson and Knox." This act was passed June 11, 1792, and describes with minute particularity that part of the boundaries of the old counties affected by it, as well as those of the new counties created. The act appoints Charles McClung and James Maberry to run and mark certain parts of the lines, and Alexander Outlaw and Joseph Hamilton to run and mark the other parts. It also directs that the Courts of Pleas and Quarter Sessions for Knox county be held at Knoxville, for the ensuing year, on the third Mondays of January, April, July and October, and for Jefferson county at the house of Jeremiah Matthews, on the fourth Mondays of the same months, "for the administration of justice."

The second ordinance passed by the same authority is one the example of which it were well we had followed, but, alas! we have not. This ordinance, in a preamble, recites that, "whereas, doubts have arisen whether the several Courts of Pleas and Quarter Sessions in this Territory have by the laws of North Carolina authority to levy taxes for building or repairing court houses, prisons and stocks in the said counties respectively, pay jurors and defray contingent expenses; and whereas, it is necessary that these doubts shall no longer exist"; and then proceeds to authorize and empower the courts to levy and collect a tax for the purposes named—not to issue bonds, and entail their payment, with interest, upon future generations.

The ordinance provides that the tax so levied and collected by the several counties shall not exceed, in any one year, more than fifty cents on each poll, nor more than seventeen cents on each hundred acres of land.

Wise legislators were William Blount, David Campbell and Joseph Anderson, who constituted the legislative authority. Their example was followed, after Tennessee was admitted into the Union, by the general assemblies elected by the people, for a very long period, so that, whenever money was appropriated or a county authorized to make any expenditures, the same act required the county authorities to levy a tax, collect it and pay up, instead of piling up debt. Those who wish to know how it was that Tennessee made such rapid strides in the production of statesmen, the building up of a name, the development of her natural resources, and advancement in education and the very highest order of civilization, for the first half century of her existence, have but to study the legislative history of that period.

"The Governor, Legislative Council and House of Representatives of the Territory of the United States of America South of the river Ohio" passed an act, September 30, 1794, entitled "An Act for the relief of such persons as have been disabled by wounds, or rendered incapable of procuring for themselves and families subsistence in the military service of the territory, and providing for the widows and orphans of such as have died."

The act provides that persons of the description mentioned in the caption must apply to and establish their right to an allowance, under the act, before the county court; that the county court shall make an allowance "adequate to their relief for one year—which allowance shall be continued for the succeeding year and so long as such court shall certify such person to continue under the description aforesaid"; that when such certificate was "countersigned by the Governor and President of the Council and Speaker of the House of Representatives, together with their order or certificate for the said allowance, it shall be a sufficient voucher to any sheriff, collector or treasurer paying the same, in the settlement of their public accounts."

On August 26, 1776, Congress promised, by a resolution, to the officers and soldiers of the army and navy who might be disabled in the service, a pension, to continue during the continuance of their disabilities.

On June 7, 1785, Congress recommended that the several states should make provision for the army, navy and militia pensioners resident with them, to be reimbursed by Congress.

On September 29, 1789, an act was passed providing that the military pensions which had been granted and paid by the states, respectively, in pursuance with the foregoing acts to invalids who were wounded and disabled during the late war, should be paid by the United States from the fourth day of March, 1789, for the space of one year.

The act of March 26, 1790, appropriated the sum of $96,-979.72 for paying pensions which may become due to the invalids.

The act of April 30, 1790, provides for one-half pay pensions to soldiers of the regular army disabled while in line of duty; and the act of July 16, 1790, provides that the military pensions which have been granted and paid by the states respectively shall be continued and paid by the United States from the fourth day of March, 1790, for the space of one year.

There were several other similar acts providing for the yearly payment of pensions, but the first general act which made a regular provision for the pensioning of commissioned and noncommissioned officers, musicians, soldiers, marines and seamen, disabled in the actual service of the United States, and in line of duty, by known wounds received during the Revolutionary war, was the act approved on March 10, 1806, which provided by its terms that it should remain in force for and during the space of six years from the passage thereof, and no longer; but it was subsequently revived and kept in force by the acts of April 25, 1812, May 15, 1820, February 4, 1822, and May 24, 1828.

And so it appears, that the "Governor, Legislative Council and House of Representatives of the Territory of the United States of America, south of the river Ohio," passed an act unconditionally and permanently pensioning disabled soldiers and militiamen, and the *widows* and *orphans* of such as had died from wounds, twelve years before such an act was passed by the Congress of the United States.

It would not be in keeping with the main purpose of this modest effort to catch up and put together in their proper places some dropped stitches in Tennessee history, to go into an examination in detail of the various acts passed by the legislative authority of the territorial government and by the earliest sessions of the general assembly of the state. Believing, however, that it may be profitable, at this time, to bring into public view some of the great doctrines, principles and policies that seem to have guided our early legislators, as gathered from what they did, they will be briefly mentioned, with date, substance, objects, etc.

The first of the policies indicated was that counties and municipalities should not contract interest-bearing debts and postpone their payment for a long period of years. This policy was fixed and not deviated from; for in every act which authorized a county or municipality to expend money for the

erection of public buildings of any kind, or for any other purpose, such county or municipality was also required to levy a
tax to pay for it; and, to prevent extravagance or the erection
of a building or buildings for public uses not required, the act
fixed a limit in excess of which tax should not be levied or collected. Was this because they were wiser than we are? No.
They read the constitution, took an oath to support it, and
found that it said, as it does now, that "the general assembly
shall have power to authorize the several counties and incorporated towns in this state to impose taxes for county and corporation purposes respectively"; and they had not then become
wise enough to construe the true meaning out of this provision,
and make it mean that the general assembly shall have power
to authorize counties and incorporated towns to borrow money
and issue promises and obligations to pay it ten, twenty or
thirty years after date, with interest payable semi-annually.
If some holder of such promises to pay, or of bonds issued by
a county or an incorporated town or city, should be called upon
to point out that provision in our constitution which gives power
to the general assembly to authorize a county or municipality
to enter into and deliver such obligations, what section, clause,
line or word could be found to make such bonds legal, valid
and binding?

They had the "fee question," the "school question," public
roads, the regulation of private corporations, the "gold" or
"specie contract" question, all to deal with; and they dealt
with all of them prior and up to the year 1801, taking hold of
and settling these complicated, vexatious problems in a courageous and statesmanlike way.

The fee act, passed in April, 1796, not only regulated the
compensation of public officers, but fixed the fees of attorneys
in civil suits, from "twelve dollars and fifty cents in any suit

in equity," down to "one dollar and twenty-five cents in any appeal from the judgment of a justice of the peace to the county courts." The fees allowed attorneys were specified in each character of the various suits, the greatest sum allowed being twelve dollars and fifty cents.

Two acts, however, ought to have special prominence given to them in Tennessee at this particular time (March, 1897). One of these, bearing on the subject of "gold" or "specie contracts," with the cunning methods used to ultimately accomplish the repeal of the most important section in it, is here given in full:

An act respecting dollars and cents, and contracts, and the manner of keeping accounts, so far as respects the currency in which contracts shall be made and accounts kept. Passed January 5th, 1799.

SEC. 1. *Be it enacted by the General Assembly of the State of Tennessee,* That all judgments and verdicts in courts of record, and by justices of peace out of court, shall be rendered in dollars and cents, or such parts thereof as the nature of the case may require; and all executions thereon and all bills of costs shall issue accordingly.

SEC. 2. *Be it enacted,* That from and after the first day of January, One thousand eight hundred, all accounts shall be kept, and contracts made where money is stipulated for, in dollars and cents, or such parts thereof as the nature of the case may require; and all accounts kept or contracts entered into, where money is stipulated for, other than is by this act directed, shall be void and not recoverable by law.

By an act passed October 23, 1799, the second section of the foregoing act was suspended "until the next stated General Assembly." At the next general assembly, November 10, 1801, this second section was again suspended "until the next stated General Assembly." At the next succeeding general assembly, October 25, 1803, the following act was passed:

Chap. 60. An Act to repeal *part* [italics mine] of the second section of an Act entitled An Act respecting dollars and cents, contracts and the manner of keeping accounts, passed January the fifth, 1799.

1. *Be it enacted by the General Assembly of the State of Tennessee,* That so much of the second section of the above

recited Act that requires all accounts kept or contracts entered into, where money is stipulated for, other than are by said Act directed, shall be void and not recoverable by law, is hereby repealed, any law to the contrary notwithstanding, *except* as respects accounts kept by *merchants, physicians* and *innkeepers* [italics mine].

2. *Be it enacted*, That this Act shall be in force after the first day of September next.

October 3, 1805, another act, of one section only, was passed, as follows:

An Act to repeal the second section of an Act respecting dollars and cents, accounts, contracts, &c.

Be it enacted, That the second section of the before recited Act, passed on the fifth day of January, in the Year of Our Lord One thousand seven hundred and eighty-nine, be and the same is hereby repealed, anything to the contrary notwithstanding.

The original act passed in January, 1799, was intended to remedy two evils. The first, but not the chief one, was to put a stop to the keeping of accounts, the taking of notes or the making of any kind of contract where payment in money was stipulated for, in pounds, shillings and pence, and to compel the use in all such obligations of the terms dollars and cents; and to more effectually enforce this, the act prohibited courts from rendering judgments, making out bills of costs or issuing executions for anything but dollars and cents. The second evil the act, in its original form and provisions, had forever cut up by the roots was the "specie" account or contract—that is to say, the shrewd keepers of accounts and money-lenders would embody in the account, note or other obligation, where money was stipulated for, the term "specie." If it was an account, it would be opened something like this: "Spruce McCay, in account with Ephraim Dunlap—specie"; or if a note, due-bill or other obligation, the term "specie" usually followed the "promise to pay" or the statement of the amount contracted to be paid or acknowledged to be due.

To the close student of the methods which are usually employed by the artful and designing, these several acts are amusing—first suspending a particular section, then suspending it again, then repealing part of it, and finally accomplishing the repeal of the whole section. Now, note. The first repealing act excepted from its provisions "merchants, physicians and inn-keepers"; that is, the repealing act was so artfully worded as to leave the original act in full force against the three classes mentioned—about the only people who transacted any business of consequence and who required payment in money at that time. These could not make any contract, or keep an account, for payment in "specie"—they must accept payment in the currency of the times. The system of barter, at this period, between the agricultural class and the blacksmith, cooper, wagonmaker, shoemaker, etc., was such that accounts between them were so kept as to be payable in the products of each, and not in money—no money ever being passed between them or expected. Thus, this first repealing act, stripped of the film that shrouded it, simply left the original act in full force against everybody that it could have affected, except one poor fellow—or one class of poor fellows—the man or men who had a little bit of money to loan on a note with "undoubted personal security" or secured by mortgage.

This first repealing act was "class legislation" so rank and rotten that the poor fellows who had money to loan—and who had it passed—became, no doubt, exceedingly solicitous for the well-being, prosperity and "business interests" of the "merchants, physicians and inn-keepers" and therefore came forward at the next meeting of the general assembly, in 1805, with an act repealing the whole of the second section of the original act; and then they breathed easy and praised the Lord because they had entirely relieved the "merchants, physicians and inn-keepers" of this odious act, which had for its object the prevention of requiring payment in "specie" where money should be stipulated for.

This last full and final repealing act deserves to be further noted, and to be remembered with reverence—so to speak—for the reason that it is the first act passed in Tennessee in which the term "in the year of our Lord" is used. What an intellectual treat it must have been to hear the man (not the member of the general assembly) who prepared this last repealing act, explaining its provisions to the members of the general assembly, and pointing out to them the great benefits that were to accrue to the " merchants, physicians and inn-keepers" of the country by its passage; and also to note with what reverential humility he bowed his head, and with what unction he read, " 'in the year of our Lord,' who has put it into my mind and heart to prepare this great measure and ask you to pass it"; and (aside) "has also made me a shining light in the church and the community"—while, all the time and every minute, his greedy, covetous little soul was becoming more contracted, and visions of dollars or pounds in "specie" were blinding him to the great truth that it would be easier for a camel to go through the eye of a needle than for such as he ever to enter the domain of "our Lord," where "specie" is used only to pave streets.

The county court records at Jonesboro show that, early in the nineties of the last century, slave-holders were emancipating their slaves.

On October 2, 1797, an Act was passed by the General Assembly of Tennessee entitled, "An Act to confirm the emancipation of a black man named Jack." The preamble recites that, "Whereas at July sessions One thousand seven hundred and ninety seven, John Stone, of Knoxville, in the State of Tennessee did apply to the County Court of Knox, for a license to emancipate, and forever set free a certain negro man slave, named Jack," etc., "which license hath issued to said John Stone, and whereas the said John Stone, on the thirty-first day of August 1797 . . . did emancipate, discharge and forever set free from all manner of servitude and slavery whatever, the said negro Jack." The Act then confirms the emancipation, and confers upon the liberated slave "the name of John Saunders."

On November 13, 1801, the General Assembly passed an act, entitled "An Act empowering the county courts to emancipate slaves," the preamble of which recites that, "Whereas the number of petitions presented to this legislature, praying the emancipation of slaves, not only tend to involve the state in serious evils, but are also productive of great expense. For remedy whereof, *Be it enacted*," &c. The act then proceeds to confer power and authority upon the county courts generally to emancipate slaves upon the petition and request of the owners, and directs the clerks of such courts to record such proceedings and make out and issue to the emancipated slaves a certificate of emancipation. These old records will explain why it was that, twenty and twenty-five years later, the "Manumission Intelligencer" and "The Emancipator" were published at Jonesboro and the "Genius of Universal Emancipation" at Greeneville. They show another fact, viz., that long before *Elihu Embree,** Benjamin Lundy, William L. Garrison

---

*Thomas Jefferson Wilson, an aged, intelligent and respected citizen, now nearly blind, living at Chesterton, in Washington county, Tenn., writing to me, April 1, 1897, among other things, says: "In the spring of 1833 I went to live with Elijah Embree [brother of Elihu], and continued to reside with him until his death, in 1846. During this time I had access to all his books and papers, and I found a copy of 'The Emancipator.' I hunted up all of the numbers that had been issued,

LIMESTONE HOUSE. 1780.

Home of Elihu Embree, the founder and editor of the first abolition paper published in the United States. Erected by his brother, Thomas Embree, about five miles west of Jonesboro, now near Telford's Station, on Southern Railway. From a photograph taken in April, 1897.

and Harriet Beecher Stowe began the agitation of the abolition of slavery—in theory—in the public press, these people were not only *thinking*, but *acting*, on the subject—the great question that ultimately shook the pillars of the American republic, and earthquaked a continent when the shock of war came—these people were not only teaching but practising emancipation. It would not only be unpatriotic, but filial impiety in the descendants of those people, to allow without protest their fame to diminish, and their views, deeds and accomplishments to be taken from them and credited to others.

It must not be. It was easy indeed, for Embree, Lundy and others to drop in, twenty to twenty-five years later, and join them in the advocacy of the policy of emancipating slaves, when they found, or had heard before coming to the country, that manumission societies had been in existence for near a quarter of a century before, and when the county court records disclosed the fact that these people were practising what they advocated, and when petitions to the general assembly of the state from the various counties "praying the emancipation of slaves" were so numerous that they were about to involve the state in serious evils by turning irresponsible persons loose upon society and also entailing great expense.

The reader, must not however, confuse the policy advocated and *practised* by those people of emancipation or of manumitting their slaves, with the doctrine of forcible abolition, or of

and had James Dilworth of Jonesboro to bind them in book form. Elihu Embree claimed [in 'The Emancipator'] that his paper was the first paper ever published in the United States wholly in the interest of emancipation. It was a monthly paper, and the first number was published in 1820, during which year Embree died, and the paper ceased. The first movement that I know of in Tennessee in the interest of emancipation was among the Quakers. They organized a society on Lost Creek, in Jefferson county, from which sprang many similar societies all over East Tennessee. Charles Owens, Benjamin Lundy and a great many others who were emancipationists moved [from Eastern Tennessee] to Ohio between 1815 and 1820."

With reference to this subject of the first abolition paper, see an interesting note on Elihu Embree, in the interpretation of the "Centennial Dream," in the appendix to this volume.

freeing slaves by legislative enactment, without the consent of the owner. Petitions, with nearly two thousand signers or names to them, coming from all settlements in the state (territory) were presented to the Constitutional Convention in 1796, asking that a provision be embodied in the constitution prohibiting slavery in the state after the year 1864. This was the voice of prophecy coming up out of the *Western Wilderness*.

True philanthrophy liberates its own slaves, and not other people's without their consent.

The first private corporation chartered by the general assembly of Tennessee was the ''Nolichucky River Company,'' November 10, 1801. Its objects are briefly stated to be ''to clear out and remove from the bed or channel of so much of the river Nolichucky as shall be within the limits of Washington, Greene and Jefferson counties, all and every obstruction which in any way impede or hinder the navigation of the same.'' The tenth section of the act is as follows:

Be it enacted, That three custom houses be established on said river, for the purpose of receiving toll, in such places as the said Nolichucky River Company may think expedient; and any boat, craft or other vessel, entering in above the upper custom house shall pay at the rate of one dollar per ton; any boat, craft or other vessel, entering between the upper custom house and the second below, shall pay at the rate of seventy-five cents per ton; and any boat, craft or other vessel, entering in between the second custom house and the third, shall pay at the rate of fifty cents per ton.

It is worth the time of the curious to read the whole of this act, as it is not probable that another like it can be found in the statute law of any other state.

Another act deserving our attention is one passed by the third general assembly, creating the second private corporation chartered in Tennessee. What a model it was and is for the guidance of all future general assemblies, and how free we

would be today from the many questions that now vex courts
and legislative bodies, if we had only followed this wise precedent. But we have not; our "swollen estimate of our own
pre-eminence" seems to have so beclouded our minds as to cut
off vision in both directions: too proud and stiff-necked to look
back and study the example and teachings of our fathers, and
too weak-minded, with all our boasting, to see a single span of
life into the future, we have lost that which they, in their far-
reaching mental grasp, held on to in the charter—control and
regulation of private corporations by means of commissions
appointed by state authority and compensated by the corporation, these provisions being part and parcel of the charter.
The act referred to was passed November 14, 1801, and incorporated the Cumberland Turnpike Company—nothing but a
little turnpike company, to build a road or public highway
"from the district of Hamilton, across the Cumberland mountains to the district of Mero": but these backwoods pioneers,
who (as we, their offspring, have supposed) did not know how
to spell "railroad," "commission," "regulation," "freight,"
etc., actually had sense and foresight enough, without books
and court decisions bearing on the subject to guide them, to
embody in this second charter of a private corporation granted
in Tennessee provisions as follows:

1. It might make by-laws, rules and regulations not incon-
sistent with the laws of the state.

2. It must "measure and mile-mark" the whole road, "erect
bridges and causeys" (causeways?), dig and level fields, hills
and mountains to the width of fifteen feet, and maintain and
keep the road in good order and repair.

3. The life of the franchise is limited to a period of ten
years.

4. The corporation is required to execute a bond, in the sum

6

of two thousand dollars, with approved security, for keeping the road in safe condition and good repair.

5. The Governor shall appoint three commissioners, and they or either of them shall review and examine the condition of the road once in six months, and report its condition to the Governor.

6. The company, on the completion of the road, is required to report to the Governor that the road has been completed in accordance with the charter requirements.

7. Thereupon, the commissioners are to view and examine the road, and if they report to the Governor that the road has been completed in accordance with the true intent and meaning of the charter, the Governor will then issue a license to the company, permitting it to erect gates and collect toll.

8. The toll that shall be demanded and received from the various kinds of vehicles, live stock, footmen, etc., is prescribed by the charter.

9. It provides that, if any person shall sustain any damage on account of being detained by the keepers of said turnpikes, or on account of the road being out of repair, such person shall have an action against the company for the damages sustained.

10. It fixes the compensation of the commissioners at two dollars per day while necessarily employed, which shall be paid by the corporation.

11. It requires the road to be completed on or before the first day of September, 1802, in default of which all rights granted by the charter are forfeited.

This charter takes up one page and two-thirds of another page of the acts as published, and is embodied, caption and all, in eighty-one printed lines; and yet almost every conceivable phase of the questions which have arisen between the people and such corporations, to annoy both and vex courts and general assemblies, are fully covered in this short charter, either in specific words, terms and provisions, or in the true intent and meaning of the whole.

Some features of this charter deserve more than a passing notice. One, which limited the life of the corporation to ten years, is in keeping with and conformity to the great doctrine announced in the twenty-third paragraph of the "declaration of rights" appended to and adopted as part of the state constitution in 1796, that "perpetuities and monopolies are contrary to the genius of a free state, and shall not be allowed": therefore they limited the life of this "monopoly" to ten years. As private citizens, the men who composed the general assembly believed in this doctrine; and, as representatives of the people, they stuck to it with a firmness and manliness worthy to be followed by all future legislative bodies.

Another feature of this second charter, which should have commended it as a model in form and substance to future general assemblies, is the retention in its face of the right and power of the state to regulate and control the road, in its condition with reference to the safety of the travelling public, and the services to be rendered and the charges to be made therefor, as well as to require the corporation to pay the agents of the people, who were to supervise and regulate it in these particulars.

Here again, in this second charter of a private corporation for profit, is given unmistakable evidence that these early legislators believed in and adhered to that other fundamental principle proclaimed in the "declaration of rights"—that "all power is inherent in the people, and all free governments are founded on their authority and instituted for their peace, safety and happiness; for the advancement of those ends, they have at all times an unalienable and indefeasible right to alter, reform or abolish the government in such manner as they may think proper." They had probably not learned, so early, that it would ever be insisted by anyone that the government could bring into existence a creature greater and more powerful than the creator; but fearing, no doubt, that such a claim might be set up, they put in the face of this charter an answer to any such pretence. It had not probably been intimated, at that early day, that a government which the people, in the exercise of their inherent power, could alter, reform or abolish at their pleasure, could nevertheless by its legislature bring into existence an invisible, intangible, incorporeal entity which the people could neither control nor destroy, although they have the power to do both with reference to the creator of such entity; still, they said in the charter that all power is inherent in the people, and you take the rights, privileges and franchises granted, subject to their power to control and regulate your operations, and your dealings with and relations to the public.

Two other features of this charter deserve to be thoughtfully considered. The first is that the corporation is made liable, in the face of its charter, for damages sustained by any person who shall be detained by the keepers of the turnpikes or the bad condition of the road. Under the language of the section, the liability is fixed and absolute, the plaintiff having to prove only two facts in any case: the fact that he was detained, and the amount of damage sustained—this was all; he did not have to prove negligence, or carelessness, ordinary or gross. The other feature is that which required the corporation to give a bond, with approved security, conditioned for keeping the road in good repair. The corporation might become insolvent, go into the hands of a receiver, come out again under a new organization, load up again with mortgages first, second and third, stock itself again and issue first and second preferred and common, and then collapse again; but the bond which this charter required this corporation to give, and the security thereon, could not be cancelled, or touched by anyone except one who had sustained damages by reason of being detained by the keepers of the gates or the road being out of repair. The corporation might dissolve, become bankrupt, go out of business —but the bond and security remained.

What a monument is this charter, granted to a private corporation for profit, to the wisdom and far-reaching foresight of the pioneer statesmen who framed and granted it; and how unfortunate it is, for both the people and for the corporations, that subsequent general assemblies in Tennessee have not engrafted its principles upon all charters since granted to private corporations.

" History repeats itself " only when and where human nature parallels itself: have legislative statesmen duplicated themselves in Tennessee?

CHAPTER VI.

IN November, 1784, the general assembly of North Carolina, at Newbern, divided the district of Morgan, which had theretofore included all of the state "west of the mountains," and erected Washington, Sullivan, Greene and Davidson counties into a "Superior Court of Law and Equity" district, by the name of "Washington." From 1784 to 1788 all of the territory west of the Cumberland mountains was included in Davidson and Sumner counties, then the only organized counties in what is now Middle and West Tennessee. The population of Davidson county had so increased and extended westward from Nashville by the fall of 1788 that the general assembly of North Carolina, at Fayetteville, in November of that year, divided Davidson county by a line "beginning on the Virginia line now Kentucky, thence south along Sumner county to the dividing ridge between Cumberland river and Red river, thence westwardly along said ridge to the head of the main south branch of Sycamore creek, thence down the said branch to the mouth thereof, thence due south across Cumberland river to Davidson county line." All that part of Davidson county west of this line was erected into a new county, which was named "Tennessee." Tennessee county, therefore, included all of the territory now within the limits of Montgomery, Robertson, Dickson, Houston and Stewart, and parts of Hickman, Humphreys and Cheatham. The county seat of Tennessee county was fixed at Clarksville.

By another act of the general assembly of North Carolina, at Fayetteville, in November, 1788, the counties of Davidson,

Sumner and Tennessee were erected into a new district for the holding of "Superior Courts of Law and Equity" therein. When this act forming the new district west of the Cumberland mountains was on its third and final reading, the Speaker called on the author of the bill for the name with which the blank left for that purpose was to be filled. James Robertson and Robert Hays were the members from Davidson, and one of them was the author of the bill providing for the new district. It is a matter of history that, in answer to the Speaker's call for the name of the new district, James Robertson arose and suggested "Mero." He evidently gave the name as it is pronounced, without spelling it for the benefit of the clerk, and the latter evidently recorded it phonetically; and thus the name of the new district went upon the official record as "Mero," which is the correct pronunciation, instead of "Miro," which is the correct orthography. The error, once committed, was perpetuated; and "Mero" it continued to be, not only in contemporary records and legal documents, but in subsequent histories. *

The name as suggested by Robertson was adopted without open objection. It is probable that some of the leading spirits in the assembly had been made acquainted with the motive which prompted the selection of the name, while others, without any knowledge, opinion or preference, simply followed the leaders in accepting it. There were, however, some members who knew some things, but not everything, in connection with this name; and, on reflection, after the name had been adopted, they took offence at the selection, and it was discussed, not in the general assembly, but at the taverns and boarding-houses, with spirit and much feeling. They said that it was strange and unexampled that the name of an officer of a foreign government, who was not and had never been in our service, should

* Haywood, Ramsey, Putnam and Phelan unanimously and invariably so spell it.

be given to a political division of our country and perpetuated
on our public records.   They wished to know what this meant.*
They knew, they said, that Don Estevan Miro was a colonel in
the Spanish army, that he was also "Governor of Orleans,"
and they had heard that he was a very kind-hearted, agreeable
gentleman; but so were scores of other foreigners, not to mention the names of the many loyal and distinguished citizens of
the United States who had not been honored with any such
mark of popular esteem.   Why, said they, select a Spaniard
already very distinguished, and at the very time when that nation unjustly withholds from us the free navigation of the Mississippi river, and when this very Don Estevan Miro is the instrument chosen by the Spanish king and court to guard the
waters and mouth of the Mississippi and exclude us from its
use?   And this is not all; why, they continued, should a Spanish official be so honored during the very same year when Spain
was demanding of the Congress that the United States should
relinquish the navigation of the Mississippi for a period of at
least twenty-five years—a measure which, if acceded to, would
completely break up and ruin all of the settlements in Kentucky
and on the Cumberland?   Still more, this mark of respect was
shown to a Spanish soldier and governor at a time when the
boatmen from the upper Mississippi, Ohio and Cumberland, if
they dared to float their flatboats down the Mississippi to
Natchez or New Orleans with their tobacco and other products,
were subjected by the Spanish to the most outrageous fines and
extortions, in the shape of duties imposed for the use of a great
river, and also to seizure and sometimes to imprisonment.   Last
but not least, said they, this very Don Estevan Miro is at this
very time negotiating and intriguing with certain persons in
Kentucky and Cumberland, with a view of coming to terms

* Haywood's History of Tennessee.

upon which Kentucky and the Cumberland country will become part of and submit to the government of Spain. Truly, it did appear rather cloudy.

These various phases of the subject, and the situation of affairs at that particular time, gave to the tavern-talkers a wide field for speculation and conjecture, as well as alarm. The truth is, the correspondence and communications alleged to have passed between Governor Miro and certain citizens of Kentucky and the Cumberland country, about this time, would read rather curiously if offered in court to vindicate the Kentucky and Cumberland citizens from a charge of disloyalty to the United States. Col. Robertson, however, said nothing but "Miro"; and he subsequently demonstrated that he knew what he was saying.

It is suggested—and this is probably the correct view—that the main purpose of these persons in Kentucky and Cumberland who were in correspondence with Governor Miro was, in view of their unanswered appeals to Congress for help and protection, "if the federal Union can not give aid and protection to us in life, liberty and property, and also secure to us the free and peaceable exercise of the right to navigate the Mississippi river with our products, why then, Spain having promised all this, we will unite our fortunes with the Spanish." They knew that whoever could keep the Indians at peace with them, and at the same time control New Orleans and the navigation of the Mississippi, was the absolute arbiter of their destiny, inasmuch as, without the right to use the Mississippi, there was no market they could reach with their products.

August 26, 1779, Galvez, then governor civil and military and intendant of Louisiana, appointed, as third in command in the campaign which he was about to undertake against the British, Don Estevan Miro, with the rank of lieutenant-colonel.

Congress observed with satisfaction the rupture between Great
Britain and Spain; and, in the fall of 1779, sent a minister to
the Spanish court, with instructions to negotiate a treaty of alliance, and particularly to insist on the free navigation of the Mississippi river.   To this the court of Spain responded: " We are
disposed to acknowledge the independence of the United States,
and to enter into a treaty of alliance and commerce with you;
but if you wish us to consent to your admission into the great
family of nations, you must subscribe to the right of Spain to
the exclusive navigation of the Mississippi, and consent to our
taking possession of both the Floridas and of all the territory
extending from the left bank of that river to the back settlements of the former British provinces, according to the proclamation of 1763."   In this proposition, strange as it may seem,
Spain was supported by France; and up to 1788, and indeed on
up to October 27, 1795, Spain did control the Mississippi.   On
this latter date, and about six months before Tennessee was admitted into the Union, after long and tedious negotiations, a
treaty was concluded between the United States and Spain, a
part of the fourth article of which reads as follows: "'And his
Catholic Majesty has likewise agreed that the navigation of the
said river Mississippi, in its whole breadth from the source to
the ocean, shall be free to only his subjects and the citizens of
the United States, unless he shall extend this privilege to the
subjects of other powers by special convention."   At the time
this treaty was entered into, Governor Miro was in Spain, in
attendance, it has been said, on the court at Madrid.   He was
then a lieutenant-general in the Spanish army, and held in great
esteem in Spain, and nothing is more probable than that his
counsel and advice on the subject of the proposed treaty were
sought.   It was entirely natural that, when asked for his views,
he should remember James Robertson, Daniel Smith and Rob-

ert Hays, the courtesy shown him and the friendly and respectful treatment which he had received from the inhabitants of the
district named in his honor, and that he should therefore favor
the concession of this right. In the very nature of things, the
district of "Mero," misspelled though it was, and the circumstances connected with and surrounding its baptism and the
man who was its sponsor, ought to and must have a place, not
only in Tennessee history, but in the true history of the United
States.

The Spaniards, constantly haunted by fear of their restless
neighbors in Kentucky and the Cumberland country, spared no
means by which they might conciliate the Indians. The chief
military officer of the Spanish, writing to the home government,
in 1786, concerning Alexander McGillivray, said: "So long as
we shall hold this chief on our side, we will have a barrier
between the Floridas and Georgia. The Indians are convinced
of the ambition of the Americans; past injuries still dwell in
their minds, with the fear that these greedy neighbors may one
day seize upon their lands. It ought to be one of the chief
policies of this government to keep this sentiment alive in the
breasts of the Indians." Alexander McGillivray was a noted
tory during the Revolution, and had taken refuge after its
close among the Creek nation. He was a man of great courage
and intelligence, entertained inveterate hostility to the whites,
and had an insatiable ambition for personal promotion. He
was in the Spanish pay, as agent of that government among
the Indians, had usurped regal authority, and was also chief of
the Talapouches. It is said that he cherished the hope of having his nation admitted into the federal compact, although he
was in the service of Spain, with the rank of colonel, and was
afterward promoted to be commissary general. This dangerous
man was under the absolute control of Governor Miro in 1788,

when the name of the latter was bestowed by Robertson on the new district. The fact that Miro had control of the Mississippi river, and at the same time almost absolute command over the Indians in the south, furnishes, it is believed, the logical explanation of the motive which prompted Robertson and Hays to compliment him by giving his name to the newly established judicial district.

In 1788 Miro was made civil and military governor and intendant of Louisiana and West Florida. In this year McGillivray wrote him that two delegates from the district of Cumberland had just visited him with proposals of peace; that they were in extremities on account of the incursions of his (McGillivray's) warriors, and would submit to whatever conditions he might impose; and, "presuming that it would please me, they added that they would throw themselves in the arms of His Majesty as subjects, and that Kentucky and Cumberland are determined to free themselves from Congress; that they no longer owe obedience to a power which is incapable of protecting them. They desired to know my sentiments on the propositions, but as it embraces important political questions, I thought proper not to divulge my views." Miro, commenting on this letter, says:

I consider as extremely interesting the intelligence conveyed to McGillivray by the deputies on the fermentation existing in Kentucky, with regard to a separation from the Union. Concerning the proposition made to McGillivray by the inhabitants of Cumberland to become the vassals of His Majesty, I have refrained from returning any precise answer.

McGillivray was no doubt, at the very time he was writing to Miro, also in the service and pay of the British; for, in April, 1788, in a letter dated at "Little Tellisee, Upper Creek Nation," and addressed to Colonels Anthony Bledsoe and James Robertson, he says, among other things:

Mr. Hackett arrived here a few Days ago and Delivered me your letter, together with one from Col. Hawkins. Agreeably to your request I will be Explicit and Candid in my answer to yours, and will not deny that my Nation had waged war against your Country for several years past, but that we had no motives of revenge, nor did it proceed from any Sense of Injurys Sustained from your people, but being warmly attached to the British, and being under their Influence, our operations were directed by them against you in common with other Americans.

The letter from which the foregoing is quoted is of considerable length. I have seen the original, with two others, and have "true and perfect copies" of all three.* That from which I have quoted above bears entirely upon the subject of a peace proposed between the Creek nation and Cumberland in the letter of Colonels Bledsoe and Robertson to which it is an answer; and there is not one word in McGillivray's letter which indicates, even remotely, that Robertson and Bledsoe had made any such proposition to him as he had communicated to Miro. Col. Robertson had written him, telling him, among other things, that a number of the settlers on Cumberland had been killed recently by his warriors—"among those unfortunate persons," says Robertson, "were my third son."

Further along in McGillivray's letter to Bledsoe and Robertson, he says: "I had received his Excel. Governor Caswell's letter and Duplicate only a short time before the unlucky affair —so that I Differed writing an answer until I could be satisfyed in my own mind that he might Depend on what I should say to him, as I abhor every Species of Duplicity, I wish not to deceive." He concludes as follows: "I have endeavored to make everything as agreeable as my Situation permits to Messrs. Hackett & Ewing"—which shows that the men named are the "two delegates from the district of Cumberland" referred to in

---

*This "big Injun" seems to have written his name as the fancy struck him. The signature to one of the letters is "McGillivray," while the other two are signed "McGilveray." All are in the same handwriting, and all are evidently autographic.

his letter to Miro; and these two letters, taken together, show what a treacherous villain and liar he was, notwithstanding his abhorrence of "every Species of Duplicity."

In April, 1789, writing to General Wilkinson of Kentucky, who was his confederate in the undertaking to separate Kentucky, Miro says:

I have just received two letters, one from Brig. Gen. Daniel Smith, dated on the 4th of March, and the other from Col. James Robertson, with date of the 11th of January, both written from the district of Miro. The bearer, Fagot [Hackett?], a confidential agent of Gen. Smith, informed me that the inhabitants of Cumberland, or Miro, would ask North Carolina for an act of separation the following fall, and that as soon as this should be obtained other delegates would be sent from Cumberland to New Orleans, with the object of placing that territory under the domination of His Majesty. I replied to both in general terms.

On the next day after writing this letter, Governor Miro wrote to Gen. Daniel Smith and Col. James Robertson, saying, among other things:

The giving of my name to your district has caused me much satisfaction, and I feel myself highly honored by the compliment. It increases my desire to contribute to the development of the resources of that province and the prosperity of its inhabitants. I am extremely flattered at your proposition to enter into correspondence with me, and I hope that it will afford me the opportunity to be agreeable to you.

These letters, messages and communications between Governor Miro and leading citizens of Miro District are more simple and straightforward than diplomatic. The reader of this part of our history, however, must keep in mind the precarious condition of the citizens of the Miro District at this period: a vast wilderness of more than two hundred and fifty miles behind them, savage Indians on both sides and the Spanish in front of them; with their state government and Congress both so weak that neither was able to extend them the slightest aid or protection—thus situated, they very naturally turned in the direction that not only had the power but gave the promise of protection and assistance. Miro, in acknowledging the compliment conveyed by bestowing his name on the new court district, said: "It increases my desire to contribute to the development of the resources of that province and the prosperity of its inhabitants." In the year 1790, the Spanish court, contrary to the advice of Governor Miro, made a formal order levying a tax or duty of fifteen per cent. on all produce or freight carried down the Mississippi river. This order so inflamed the people of Kentucky and Miro District that it had the effect feared by Miro, of practically breaking off and forever ending further negotiations between him and the people of Miro District on the subject of the Cumberland country becoming a Spanish province.

Judge Martin, in his history of Louisiana, says that, at about the period of time when these letters were passing, there were five parties in the western country—one in favor of the formation of a new republic unconnected with the United States, and a close alliance with Spain; another that wished the western part of the United States to become a portion of the province of Louisiana and to submit to the laws of Spain; a third, desirous of war with Spain, an open invasion of Louisiana and the seizure of the Mississippi and New Orleans; a fourth, proposing by a show of war to prevail on Congress to extort from Spain the right to the free navigation of the Mississippi; the fifth, as unnatural as the second, was to solicit France to procure a retrocession of Louisiana and to extend her protection to Kentucky and Cumberland.

The administration of Miro in Louisiana terminated with the year 1791. In a letter to the Spanish court, written in the previous year, asking permission to return to Spain, he says: "I

have now had the honor of serving the King, always with distinguished zeal, for thirty years and three months, of which
twenty-one years and eight months in America, until the state
of my health requires my return to Europe." He returned to
Spain, where he continued his military career, being promoted
from the rank of brigadier to that of lieutenant-general. "He
carried with him," says Judge Martin, "the good wishes and
regrets of the colonies."

The character of Miro was that of a kind-hearted, benevo-
lent, upright gentleman. Leprosy prevailed in Louisiana, and
one of Miro's first acts, on being appointed Governor, was to
erect a hospital for the unfortunate victims of that disease, on
a ridge lying between the Mississippi river and Bayou St. John,
which was called "Leper's Land." Instances were related in
which Miro would intercede with a creditor to give further time
to an unfortunate debtor, and on failing to obtain such indul-
gence, he would satisfy the debt out of his private funds. In
April, 1786, the king of Spain issued a royal order, approving
the course and conduct of Miro, who, in the preceding year,
had granted the former British subjects in Baton Rouge and
Natchez, which had been conquered by the Spanish, ample time
to sell their property, collect their debts and remove their persons and effects.

Don Estevan Miro left his name on the judicial records and
reports of Tennessee, where it remained until November 4, 1809,
when, by act of the general assembly, the state was divided
into five judicial circuits, to which the act affixed numbers instead of names. Miro District, in addition to Davidson, Sumner and Tennessee counties, included at one time the counties
of Smith, Wilson and Williamson. When "the territory of
the United States of America south of the river Ohio" was admitted into the Union as the state of Tennessee, the county of

Tennessee, at the first session of the general assembly, by an act passed April 9, 1796, was divided into Montgomery and Robertson counties. Thus the "District of Mero" and "Tennessee county" appeared on and then disappeared from the face of the map and the public records of the state of Tennessee.

The "Superior Courts of Law and Equity" for the Miro District were held in Nashville. An act of the first session of the first general assembly of Tennessee, passed April 22, 1796, recites that the court house, or the "office of the clerk and master of the District of Mero was lately destroyed by fire, and the books, records and papers thereof lost," etc., and then provides for setting up the records.

While the capital and the state treasury were located at Knoxville, there was a branch treasury kept in the Miro District at Nashville.

The present chief justice of the United States, Hon. Melville W. Fuller, in an opinion on the constitutionality of a recent law of the state of Michigan, providing for the selection of presidential electors by a vote of each congressional district separately taken, refers to an act of the general assembly of the state of Tennessee, which appointed a committee of citizens in the District of Miro and empowered it to elect presidential electors—the chief justice, as I understand him, approving both these methods as a compliance with the constitution. The act referred to is worthy of acquaintance, and I therefore embody the substance of it in this chapter, as I presume that there are very few persons familiar with its provisions. The act was passed August 8, 1796, and is as follows:

Be it enacted by the General Assembly of the State of Tennessee, that three electors shall be elected, one in the district of Washington, one in the district of Hamilton and one in the district of Mero, as directed by this Act, to elect a president and vice president of the United States, and that the said

7

electors may be elected with as little trouble as possible to the citizens.

Sec. 2nd. Be it enacted that John Carter, John Adams, and John McCollester of the County of Washington; John Rhea, John Spurgeon and Robert Allison of Sullivan County; Daniel Kennedy, Joseph Hardin and James Stinson of the county of Greene; and Richard Mitchell, John Young and Bartlet Marshall of the county of Hawkins, are appointed electors to elect an elector for that purpose for the district of Washington; John Adair, Charles McClung and Samuel Flonnagan of the County of Knox; Andrew Henderson, Josiah Jackson and Christopher Hains of the County of Jefferson; Samuel Mc-Gahey, Josiah Gist, Alexander Montgomery of the County of Sevier; and Robert Boid, William Lowry and David Caldwell of Wells Station of the County of Blount, are appointed electors to elect an elector for the purpose aforesaid for the district of Hamilton; Thomas Molloy, William Donelson and George Ridley of the County of Davidson; Kasper Mansco, Edward Douglass and John Hogan of the County of Sumner; George Nevill senior, Josiah Fort and Thomas Johnson of the late county of Tennessee, are appointed electors to elect an elector in the District of Mero, for the purpose aforesaid.

Sec. 4. The electors in this Act before named shall convene, those for the District of Washington at Jonesborough, those for the District of Hamilton at Knoxville, and those for the District of Mero at Nashville, on the Second Monday of November in the year 1796, and being so convened, they, or so many of them as shall attend on said day, proceed to elect by ballot an elector qualified as by this Act directed, for the purpose aforesaid.

The act further provides that, ''if two or more persons shall have the same number of votes, it shall be decided in the same manner as Grand Jurors are drawn for, in the Superior Courts''. —that is, the names of such persons as received the same number of votes were to be written on slips of paper and put into a box or hat; a boy under twelve years of age then drew out one of the slips, and the person whose name appeared thereon received the certificate of election.

The electors chosen received certificates of election signed by the committee, and the three electors thus chosen were directed by the act to "convene at Knoxville on the first Wednesday in December, 1796, and proceed to elect a president and vice-president of the United States."

This act, or method of selecting presidential electors, was re-enacted by the general assembly of Tennessee, October 26, 1799, for the presidential election to occur in 1800. I am not aware that this method of selecting presidential electors was ever adopted by any other state.

This seeming digression from the main subject will be pardoned, in view of the fact that Chief Justice Fuller, as I understand him, refers to the act under consideration as applicable only to the Miro District.

The method of choosing presidential electors prescribed in this act shows how implicitly the people at that time trusted their representatives, and also the confidence the representatives reposed in the judgment and patriotism of the citizen, as well as the confidence which the people then had in the honor and patriotism of each other.

CHAPTER VII.

IN many respects Andrew Jackson was the most interesting, picturesque and unique character America has produced. Scotch and Irish blood commingling in his veins, there was a perfect blend of the characteristics of both races, and in addition thereto he had some traits and besetments peculiarly his own. In his calm and restful moods, he was as tender and serene as a child, and easily accessible by the very humblest; but when the storm of passion swept over his soul, he was a flaming furnace of fury, almost wholly heedless of consequences, and as much to be feared and avoided as an enraged lion. In the face of perils he had the dauntlessness of John Knox, and was an exact counterpart of the great reformer when he threw down the gage of battle to the Roman hierarchy. A soldier by nature, he scoffed at the prescribed rules of military movements, and made his own tactics, surpassing even the Corsican prodigy in martial genius and originality, as the trained soldiers of Pakenham, who won the bloody field of Waterloo, testified involuntarily when they fled in defeat and dismay before his undisciplined militia from the gates of New Orleans.

The highest order of statesmanship wrought in him its perfect work. If he was not the founder, he was the preserver, of a great party. He was a sturdy patriot. Love of country was the controlling emotion of his great soul. The determination which animated him, crystallized in his stern pronouncement, "The federal union: it must be preserved!" crushed an incipient rebellion as a giant would crush a shell of glass.

His judicial administration was signalized by clear discernment, keen analysis, deep penetration, ready and correct decision, and an instinct to trail the sly and devious cunning of wrong and guilt.

Jackson lacked the refinements of fashion and the polished graces of the courtier, but his quick grasp of every situation and his instinctive sense of the proprieties bore him with composure and dignity through all the social ordeals through which he had to pass.   Still, in these functions he had a will and a way of his own, and little he recked whether others were pleased or affronted.

Jackson's figure, like the shadow of the Brocken, grows more colossal as we recede from it.

This is one side of Jackson's life—the sober, serious side—an unblurred career of honor, usefulness and triumph, for which the truth-loving muse of history never tires of garlanding his name with the most loving eulogies.   As is usually the case with mortals, there was a reverse side of Jackson's character. Here we find a few spots on the otherwise white flower of a blameless life.

In the years before honors thrust themselves so thick and fast upon him, he was what would now be called a "sport." The semi-civilization of the time, his rugged environment, the lack of training consequent upon the loss of his natural guardians, his absolute dependence upon himself, and his high-born spirit that could brook no control, combine to form an eloquent plea in extenuation of the few "indiscretions" that were mingled with so many commendable traits.   He loved the excitement and wild abandon of the chase, and the deep-mouthed pack's "heavy bay, resounding up the rocky way" and mountain solitudes, was sweeter music to his enraptured ear than a thunderous jumble of Dutch diapasons to a Wagnerian devotee.

Jackson was fond of adventure and games requiring daring, alertness, skill and strength, and engaged with the heartiest zeal in all the rude hilarities of pioneer life; but horse-racing was his special weakness.   At the time spoken of, he knew a great deal more about the "points" of a flyer than he did about Blackstone, the science of government or the ten command-ments.   A fleet-footed horse was his idol, and when he saw one equal or break the record made by Maggie on the night when she outstripped the witches of Kirk Alloway with fright-ened Tam O'Shanter clinging to her mane, his was the ecstacy of the swain in his earliest love.   On this "weak point" hangs an o'er-true tale, and the event gives a true insight into Jackson's character when he was at his worst.

It happened along in the eighties of the last century, when Jackson was a resident of Washington county and boarded with Christopher Taylor (familiarly known as "Kit Taylor," and grandfather of Skelton Taylor of Chattanooga), who lived, as stated in an earlier chapter, about one mile below Jones-boro, on the road to the Brown settlement.   At this time, Jackson's "weakness" was at its weakest, and horse-racing was his most delightful occupation.   He had a racer upon which he lavished his time and his affections, and which he imagined was the fastest in all the country ; and he was eager to "back his judgment" with all the means at his command. Col. Love, who lived in Greasy Cove, then a part of Wash-ington county and now of Unicoi, owned the champion flyer of the new country, having even defeated the fastest horses over in Virginia, about Wolf Hills, where Abingdon now stands.   Jackson envied Love, and was determined to rob him of his laurels and becloud the reputation of his horse.   He sent a challenge, which was promptly accepted.

The race was widely and graphically advertised.   In all the contests of equine speed, it would have no prototype in the past and no rival in the future. All upper East Tennessee was stirred into a ferment of excitement, which grew more intense every day, from the time of the announcement until the event took place. The coming horse-race became the absorbing, exclusive topic of conversation at the log-rollings, house-raisings, quiltings, distilleries, stores, school-houses, firesides, inns and before and after "meetin'." Children caught the infection from the adults, and the dogs, if they have the intelligence with which they are credited, doubtless cast knowing winks at each other when their respective owner's discussed the universal theme and speculated upon the outcome of the to-be-incomparable event.

The place selected for the race was in Greasy Cove, on the farm now owned by the Loves. Tall mountains looked down on lower heights, and these in turn on the spot to be made historic—a poem of nature, a dream of beauty in a setting of scenic grandeur, embroidered with the silver fretwork of the Nolichucky's restless billows.

The track was a half-circle, half a mile long.

The advertised day, in the summer or early fall of 1788, came at last, and with it the popular excitement pitched to the highest tension. And such a heterogeneous mass as swarmed into that sequestered valley—the old, the young, farmers, workers in wood and iron, lawyers, doctors, saints, sinners, and even preachers; on foot and horseback, singly, in groups and in vast cavalcades, from Washington, Greene, Hawkins, Sullivan, and from the Wolf Hills of Virginia. Civilization had not yet reached a sufficient development to produce a "moonshiner," but "the rosy" flowed as copiously as if some magician had changed the neighboring streamlets into the crystal elixir, and the number of fisticuffs was in proportion to its consumption. As was the custom of the day, the fellows "spilin' for a fight" stripped to the waist line and fought in a ring, and when one cried, "Take him off!" the mill ended, the bitten, gouged and bleeding combatants "made up," washed, dressed, and sealed the pact of peace with a drink of whiskey from the same gourd. The men who met at Sycamore shoals, followed "the sword of the Lord and of Gideon" across the Alleghanies under Sevier and Shelby, drove the Hessian hordes from King's Mountain and closed the final chapter of the Revolution with one of its grandest triumphs, were there. The pioneer who built his fort-cabin in the wilderness and shot the prowling savage through a chink in the wall, was there, with his faithful spouse and the rest of the family. The lovesick swain in his flax linen, with his bonnie lass in a gown of snowy cotton, who caused the mountain roses to pale with envy as she glided like a sylph among them, was there also. But the horse-race overshadowed everything else in interest and importance.

Jackson had been training his horse for months in advance in "Kit" Taylor's neighborhood, and the racer knew his master's imperious will perfectly. He "smelt the battle afar off," and perhaps at the same time "danger in the tainted air"; but when the test came, the determination to be first under the string thrilled every fiber and sinew in his lithe and wiry body.

The betting was fast and furious, and the reckless readiness of the gamblers, following the example of the contestants, to risk all on their favorite steed, would have taken away the breath of even the "plunger" of today. Guns, furs, iron, clothing, cattle, horses, negroes, crops, lands and all the money procurable were staked on the result. No "boom" period in that section saw so much property change hands in so short a time.

A week or ten days before the race, Jackson was overtaken
by a serious disappointment.   His jockey, a negro boy belonging to Taylor, was taken down with a violent fever.   Jackson
announced his determination to ride the race himself, and Love
readily agreed to the proposition.   When this arrangement became known, the throng became delirious with enthusiasm and
delight.   The judges, who had been selected after a good deal
of finesse and some wrangling, were stationed half and half at
each end of the semicircular track.   Jackson appeared on his
restless and impatient flyer, with a haughty air of confidence
and self-possession, the rival steed prancing at his side, under
the control of a born jockey, who well knew the responsibility
resting upon him and how to act his part on the momentous
occasion.   They were started with a shout that shook the azure
vault above and reverberated in answering echoes from the surrounding mountains.   The horses were marvels of symmetry
and beauty, and in fine condition for speed and endurance.   At
the word "Go!" they shot out on the smooth track as if they
had been hurled from two monster mortars.   On they sped,
neck and neck.   The jockey was the hazy outline of a boy
printed on the air: Jackson rode as if he were part of his spec-
tral horse.   The yells of the onlookers packed around the cres-
cent course would have drowned the blending screams of a hundred steam-whistles.   All at once, the Love horse spurted ahead.
The partisans of Jackson got their breath in gasps.   The victor
whizzed under the string like an arrow, leaving Old Hickory to
make the goal at his leisure.   If Jackson's horse was a wind-
splitter that left a blue line behind him, Love's was the same as a
belated streak of lightning chasing a hurricane that had outrun
it.   Just for a moment there was the deep, ominous hush that
precedes the crash of the tempest; then a pandemonium of
noise and tumult that might have been heard in the two neigh-

boring states broke loose. It awoke the black bear from his siesta, and the frightened red deer ''sprang from his heathery couch in haste'' and sought the distant heights. The loud, long and deep profanity would have discounted the ''army in Flanders.'' Jackson was the star actor in this riot of passion and frenzy. His brow was corrugated with wrath. His tall, sinewy form shook like an aspen leaf. His face was the livid color of the storm-cloud when it is hurling its bolts of thunder. His Irish blood was up to the boiling-point, and his eyes flashed with the fire of war. He was an overflowing Vesuvius of rage, pouring the hot lava of denunciation on the Love family in general and his victorious rival in particular. Col. Love stood before this storm unblanched and unappalled—for he too had plenty of ''sand,'' and as lightly esteemed the value of life—and answered burning invective with invective hissing with the same degree of heat and exasperation. Jackson denounced the Loves as a ''band of land pirates,'' because they held the ownership of nearly all the choice lands in that section. Love retorted by calling Jackson ''a damned long, gangling, sorrel-topped soap-stick.'' The exasperating offensiveness of this retort may be better understood when it is explained that in those days women ''conjured'' their soap by stirring it with a long sassafras stick.

The dangerous character of both men was well known, and it was ended by the interference of mutual friends, who led the enraged rivals from the grounds in different directions.

It is probable that this crushing defeat, with its intense mortification and odious memories, gave Jackson a profound distaste for the turf and other time-wasting sports of pioneer life. At all events, he turned his attention to the sober and ''weightier matters'' of life, and eagerly embraced the ''tide in the affairs of men'' which led to fame and fortune, and enabled him, on the field of battle, in the forum of law, in the council hall and at the head of a great nation, to make for himself

> "One of the few, the immortal names
> That were not born to die."

The incidents and results of this celebrated horse-race did not in the least discredit Jackson in the estimation of the people where it occurred, as was shown long afterward.   While it was difficult to exaggerate the great victory gained over the British at New Orleans by Gen. Jackson, still it was somewhat exaggerated by the time the news of it reached Jonesboro. Some few days after the first account of the battle had reached the town—in a letter from a Knoxville gentleman to a friend in Jonesboro—some court day or other public occasion had caused quite a crowd to collect in town, and the gentleman who had received the letter was requested to make a public announcement of its contents to the anxious and excited populace.   This he did in front of the court-house.   The excitement was at blood heat, but perfect silence and order prevailed while the gentleman was making his speech—for such it was, as he did not actually read the letter.   The substance of the speech was that Gen. Jackson had killed the whole of the British army on the battle-field, except a few who were driven into the Mississippi river and drowned ; that he had captured all of their arms and ships, and had taken his own army on board the vessels, and was then on the high seas on his way to take possession of England.   At this point, which was the conclusion of the speech, and old man of sixty, standing near the speaker, threw his hat into the air, and jumping excitedly up and down, shouted : "Whoop-pee ! hurrah for Andy Jackson, hell and thunder !   I knowed, the day I seed him ride that hoss-race in Greasy Cove, that he could whup anybody !"

The scene that followed was without a precedent in the history
of the town, not even the return of Sevier with his conquering
heroes from King's Mountain having caused more rejoicing
and celebrating.   From and after that time, the exclamation
of Gen. Jackson's enthusiastic admirer became a saying in the
country round about; and when news of an earthquake, the
burning of a town or city, the sinking of a ship at sea with all
on board, would be told to some not over-reverent citizen, he
would exclaim, "Andy Jackson, hell and thunder!" as the only
words adquate to express his feelings on the reception of news
of such a catastrophe.

The deep-rooted, heartfelt, undying hatred of the British
which these people nursed, kept alive and handed down, may
be illustrated by the recital of a few facts which came within
my own knowledge and observation.   During the recent war
between the states, there was much said and written, at one
period, about England recognizing the independence of the
Southern Confederacy, and entering into diplomatic or friendly
relations with the Confederate government.   While this subject
was under discussion, I heard old men, who were intense in
their loyalty to the Southern cause, and who had sent their sons
all into the Confederate army, declare openly and vehemently
that, if the Southern Confederacy "made friends with the
British," they would renounce their allegiance to it and bring
their boys home; that they had rather be subjugated by the
Yankees than to conquer with the aid of "the British"!

So late as 1882–3, Sir Thomas Watson, an Englishman, spent
several months in Jonesboro, examining and negotiating for a
valuable piece of iron property in Washington county.   He
would come to my office occasionally, and would sit and talk
with me.   On one of these occasions, an old friend of mine,
some seventy years of age, came in, and I introduced him to
Sir Thomas, telling him that the latter was from England.   My

old friend sat down, but did not address a word to the gentleman to whom I had introduced him during the half or three-quarters of an hour which ensued; but I noticed him more than once looking at the Englishman very much as if he was "drawing a bead" on him along the barrel of a rifle. When Watson left the office, the old gentleman's eyes followed him. As the door closed after him, my old friend drew a breath of relief, and asked, "What's *he* doing here?" When I told him, he appeared incredulous. "I don't believe he's after any good," he said; "better have nothing to do with a Britisher. This one may be a spy. If Andy Jackson was alive, and was to hear of that man being here, I'll bet he would drive him out of this country!"

The race-horse in Greasy Cove, in the shadow of the mountain over which Jackson had crossed a few months before, and in the midst of the early settlements of Tennessee, was not the last time he appeared on horseback in the presence of his admiring and applauding countrymen. In 1833 President Andrew Jackson rode on horseback along Broadway in the city of New York, in a "roaring wave" of shouts that came from a "sea of upturned faces" which lined the whole way of his triumphal ride through the great thoroughfare of the great city, where men, women and children had gathered to get even a passing glimpse of the hero of the hour. He was then sixty-six years old, but his horsemanship, acquired in part at the celebrated race in Greasy Cove, prevented on this occasion a serious accident to the President of the United States. It was said by those who witnessed the manner in which he sat upon and controlled the spirited and frightened charger which he rode, that the horse would have dashed any other man headlong from the saddle; but Jackson was as cool and calm as he was skillful, and soon brought the animal under perfect control—as he soon afterwards did Nicholas Biddle and the United States Bank.

CHAPTER VIII.

WAIGHTSTILL AVERY was the most prominent man and the leading lawyer in Western North Carolina when Andrew Jackson came to the bar. At that time, and indeed from the time of the organization of the first court west of the Blue Ridge, Avery had the most extensive practice of any lawyer attending the courts east or west of the mountains. He began his professional life west of the Alleghanies with the organization of the first court in Washington county, and was therefore a well-known, as he was a reputable and highly respected, lawyer before Jackson's appearance there. "He was born in Norwich, Connecticut, and was educated at Princeton, from which he graduated in 1766. He was a tutor in that college for a year, when he removed to Maryland, and studied law under Littleton Dennis. He emigrated to North Carolina, and was licensed to practise law in 1769. He encouraged education and literature, and was a most devoted friend of liberty. He led the bold spirits of his day in his patriotic county, and was a member of the convention in 1775, at Mecklenburg, that declared for independence. The minutes of the proceedings show his zeal in the cause of liberty, and the confidence of his countrymen in his talents and integrity is proved by the important duties he was engaged to perform. This called down upon him the vengeance of the enemy; for, when Lord Cornwallis occupied Charlotte, the law office of Col. Avery, with all his books and papers, was burnt. In 1775, he was a delegate from Mecklenburg in the state Congress at Hillsboro which placed the state in military organization. In 1776, he was a delegate of the same to the same, which met at Halifax and formed the state constitution. He was appointed one of the signers to the proclamation bills. In 1777, he was sent by the council (of state) with orders to Gen. Williamson, at Keowee, South Carolina. He was appointed by Governor Alex. Martin (1777), with Brig.-Gen. John McDowell and Col. John Sevier, to treat with the Cherokee Indians. He was elected the first attorney general of North Carolina, in 1777, which he resigned on account of his health, and removed to Burke county in 1781, which he represented for many years, and where he, enjoying peace and plenty and the love and regard of his neighbors, died in 1821. He was at the time of his death the 'patriarch of the North Carolina bar,' and an exemplary Christian, a pure patriot and an honest man." Such is the brief account given by the North Carolina historian, Wheeler,* of the man with whom Jackson fought the duel at Jonesboro, which shows that Avery was no ordinary man.

Avery graduated from Princeton in 1766; Jackson was born March 15, 1767. Hence, Avery must have been at least twenty years older than Jackson. The records at Jonesboro show that Avery attended the various courts up to about the time Tennessee was admitted into the Union, and that he was on one or the other side of nearly all the cases in the courts held there.

More than one version of the duel, and the cause of it, have been given. I have read and heard two of these.

Parton, in his life of Jackson,† gives an account of this duel, as detailed by Col. Isaac T. Avery, son of Col. Waightstill Avery, and it would seem that this version of the affair ought to be accepted. It will be noticed, however, that Parton's account omits to state any fact or facts that caused or led

* History of North Carolina, part ii, page 56.

† Parton's Life of Jackson, I, 162.

up to the challenge—he merely states that the two attorneys were on opposing sides in a case at Jonesboro; that the cause was going rather against Jackson, that he became irritated, and that Avery rather exultingly ridiculed some legal position taken by Jackson, using language that was more sarcastic than was called for (as he afterwards admitted), which stung Jackson, who snatched up a pen, wrote a peremptory challenge on the blank leaf of a law book and delivered it then and there to Avery, by whom it was promptly accepted.

In my search after the facts, made years ago, among the old men of Washington and Sullivan counties, I ascertained that Jackson fought two duels at Jonesboro. When I began my investigation, I had never heard of any except that with Col. Avery, and therefore, when asking some one about the matter, I would say something to this effect: "What do you remember, or what have you heard, about Jackson's duel fought at Jonesboro?" The answer, four times out of five, would be: "Which one do you mean—the one with Avery, or the one fought in the hollow?" They nearly all remembered the fact that there were two duels, or said that they did; they recollected all about the duel with Avery, and that it was fought on the hill on the south side of the town (not on the north side), and that the other one was fought in "the hollow" (as it was then called) north of the town; but they could not recall the name of the man with whom the latter duel was fought, nor the cause of it. I suggested to some of them that probably there was no duel fought with pistols in the meadow or hollow, but that it must have been a plain, old-fashioned fight with fists, as I had heard that the hollow in question was a favorite place for the fisticuff champions of the time to retire to and "fight it out fair." This suggestion was invariably met with ridicule at the mere idea of Andrew Jackson fighting with anything else than a pistol, a dirk or a sword; and I gave up the duel in the hollow with much regret at not being able to learn anything at all about it, beyond the fact that Jackson did fight one there, with some one whose name they could not remember, and the cause of which they had heard but could not recall.

The account of the duel between Jackson and Avery, as given me and as I heard it given to others, twenty, twenty-five and as far back as thirty years ago, by very old native-born citizens, agrees in the following particulars with that given by others: Jackson and Avery were opposing counsel in a suit being tried in the afternoon; the case was going apparently against Jackson's view and client; Jackson was exerting himself in an effort to escape from authorities relied on by Avery; and the latter did ridicule severely some legal position taken by his opponent. If, however, the account given me be a true one, as I have every reason to believe that it is, there is much that must be interlined in or added to the foregoing, although it can be done briefly.

Avery's favorite authority was "Bacon's Abridgment." This he carried with him from court to court, and from the tavern to the court house and back. It was always in his "green bag," and the latter, when not in his saddle-bags, was in his hand or swinging from his arm. The book was carefully wrapped up in a piece of buckskin, to preserve it from wear. Avery quoted from and referred to "Bacon's Abridgment" in every case and on all occasions, and of course had done so on the trial of the case out of which grew the duel; and Jackson had ridiculed Avery's pet authority, but had not said anything derogatory to his opponent as a lawyer or a gentleman. Avery, in his retort, grew sarcastic; he not only criticised legal positions taken by Jackson, but intimated pretty strongly that he did not know anything about the law of that case or of any other, and that he had much to learn before he would be justi-

8

fied in criticising a law book written by anyone. This was
enough to inflame Jackson, and it did. Jumping to his feet,
he exclaimed: "I may not know as much law as there is in
Bacon's Abridgment, but I know enough not to take illegal
fees!" Avery at once turned on Jackson, and demanded fiercely
to know whether he meant to charge him with taking illegal
fees. Jackson answered, "I do, sir," and started to say more;
but Avery, pointing and shaking his finger at his adversary,
hissed through his teeth, "It's as false as hell!" whereupon
Jackson immediately sat down, picked up a law book, tore a
blank leaf from it, wrote a challenge, delivered it to Avery,
bowed to him ceremoniously, and walked out of the court house.
Avery seated himself, wrote an acceptance of the challenge,
walked out of the court house and, meeting John Adair, requested him to act as his second, and to deliver his note to
Jackson. The latter, in the mean time, had met a friend,
whom he asked to act as his second, and to whom he said that
he did not wish to kill Avery; that Avery had interrupted him
without hearing all that he had intended to say, which was that
he (Avery) had taken illegal fees because of his ignorance of
the latest law fixing a schedule of fees,* and not that he had
done so corruptly; but that Avery's manner and language were
such as to prevent this intended explanation, which he could
not afford to make afterward without the probability of being
suspected of fearing Avery, and that he would rather be killed
by his antagonist than suspected of cowardice. Jackson's second (whose name I was never able to ascertain) unquestionably
communicated to Adair, during the subsequent negotiations
between them as to weapons, etc., the substance of what Jackson had said; and the two seconds determined that there should
be no duel in earnest, or "shooting to kill," as one of my in-

*Attorneys' fees were then fixed by statute, in both civil and criminal cases.

formants expressed it. This agreement must have been communicated to both principals, before they left the town for the "field of honor," as subsequent events clearly indicate.

Difficulties that led to a challenge and its acceptance, in the olden times, were rarely ever adjusted before the combatants arrived on the field. The distinguished duellists followed the custom on this occasion; and, with their seconds and others who knew of the affair, went to the ground selected—the hill on the south side of Jonesboro, and not "the hollow" north of town. The distance was measured off, the principals stationed and the word given—and Jackson and Avery both fired in the air, to the great gratification of their friends.

The two principals approached each other with extended hands. While holding his recent antagonist by the hand, Jackson said: "Col. Avery, I knew that, if I hit you and did not kill you immediately, the greatest comfort you could have in your last moments would be to have 'Bacon's Abridgment' near you; and so I had my friend bring it to the ground." Thereupon, Jackson's second unrolled the package in his hand, which was about the size of a law book, and out fell a piece of old, well-cured *bacon!*

Parton, in a note appended to his account of the duel, says that there was a comic incident connected with it, which Jackson would not tell and Adair did not. The version here given was told me by three different old men, in Washington county, years ago. They were Abram Gregg, Micajah (or Michael) Hodges and John Fullmer, each of whom had been a soldier in the war of 1812, Gregg having been, I believe, a captain. The last time that I talked with Fullmer and Hodges on this subject was in 1879, and they were both clear in their recollection, without any consultation with each other, residing in different parts of the county, Fullmer on the Watauga river and Hodges on the Holston, eight miles distant.*

The foregoing version of this duel is supported by the old court records at Jonesboro. Years ago I read and copied therefrom the following entry : "Waightsell Avery having for want of Acts of Assembly Crept into an Error in Taking Two pounds instead of One pound Six Shillings and Eight pence Was by the Court freely Pardoned at his Own Request." It is also borne out by the fact that, when Jackson was President, this duel was mentioned to him by Samuel P. Carron, then a member of Congress from the district in North Carolina in which Col. Avery died, whereupon the President, according to Parton, asked Carron, "Who told you about it?" "Gen. Adair," was the answer. "Did he tell you what happened on the ground?" "No." "Well, then, I sha'n't," said Jackson, laughing. This would indicate that the duel had had some comic ending, and not a comical beginning.

The other version of the duel, which I never heard in upper East Tennessee, agrees with the one before given, except in the following particulars. It was said that, in the course of the trial, Jackson was rather getting the best of Avery, and as it was near adjourning time, and Col. Avery, strange to say, had forgotten his green bag with "Bacon's Abridgment" in it, when returning from dinner, he said to the court that he would produce next morning the authority in support of his position; that Bacon's Abridgment would show how little the opposing counsel knew about the law in the case, etc. Next morning, Jackson went into Avery's room during the latter's absence,

*Hodges died in June, 1881, at the age of eighty-six. Fullmer died in November, 1883, ninety years old. Gregg was much older than either of the others, and died early in the seventies, a very old man. There were living in the Boon's creek civil district of Washington county, after the close of the late war, as many as seven old gentlemen who had been soldiers in the war of 1812, besides others then living in different parts of the county.

took the "Abridgment" out of the green bag, and substituted a piece of bacon about the size of the book, wrapped first in paper and then in the buckskin which Avery used as a wrapper for his precious volume. When Avery came into court with his green bag, and proceeded to produce his authority, out tumbled the piece of bacon, in the presence of the court and the lawyers, as well as the spectators who had been invited to witness the fun. This practical joke so incensed Avery that he challenged Jackson on the spot; the challenge was accepted, and the combatants immediately proceeded to the duelling ground, fired at each other, both missing, whereupon each expressed himself satisfied, and the affair ended. This latter version does not accord with what Jackson said to Carron about the comic incident, when he asked if Adair had told him what happened *on the ground*—not at the court house or before the duel.

I gathered from the old men alluded to above that public sentiment, as they understood, was rather with Avery at the time of the duel, as the people had more confidence in his law knowledge than that of "young Jackson;" but they all believed both of them to be brave and honest, although Jackson was "a little too fractious."

Did Jackson fight another duel at Jonesboro? I do not know; but it is certain that the three old gentlemen whom I have named, as well as others, asserted most positively that he did. When asked whom the duel was fought with, when it occurred, what caused it, etc., they could not remember; but they all agreed that the affair took place in the "long meadow," as it was then called (formerly the "hollow"), on the north side of town, and they all asserted that the duel with Avery was fought on the hill on the south side. Capt. Abram Gregg was of the opinion that the duel occurred in the year after

Jackson came to Jonesboro, which would fix it in 1789.   He said that Jackson hit his man, but he was not seriously wounded, and soon recovered and left the community; that Jackson was not touched.   It can be seen from this statement how the facts of the duel might have been forgotten, if it took place, as the other party to it left the country soon afterward, whereas Col. Avery continued to attend the courts of the county for years after his duel with Jackson.   This would naturally keep the matter fresh in the minds of the people, although Jackson left the county permanently about October or November, 1790.

CHAPTER IX.

RUSSELL BEAN was not distinguished alone because he was the first white child born within the limits of what is to-day the state of Tennessee: he was said to have been the most perfect specimen of manhood in the whole country, without an equal for strength, activity and physical endurance, and absolutely devoid of fear. He was a genius, also: he was a gunsmith by trade, and it was said that he could make more implements of war and other things of utility, with fewer tools, than any other man ever known in that day and country. He went to Connecticut, soon after he reached manhood, and brought back with him to the western world a supply of what were then modern tools and supplies, with which he established a kind of manufactory of arms, etc.

Bean had a flat-bottomed boat built under his directions, and with a cargo of arms of his manufacture, consisting of rifles, pistols, dirks, etc., he went alone down the Nolichucky to the Tennessee, thence to the Ohio, and down the Mississippi to New Orleans, where he remained for about two years, engaged in foot races, horse racing, cock-fighting and other sports of the times in that then great city. On returning to Jonesboro, he found his wife—who was a daughter of Col. Charles Roberson, and had borne him several children—nursing an infant. Her seducer, it was said, was a merchant of the town named Allen. Bean left the house without a word, got drunk, came back, took the baby out of the cradle, and deliberately cut off both its ears close up to its head, saying that he "had marked it so that it would not get mixed up with his children." He was arrested and, court being in session, he was tried and convicted of this act of inhuman cruelty, and sentenced, in addition to other punishment, to be branded in the palm of the hand. This was done; whereupon he immediately bit out of his hand the part containing the brand, and spat it upon the ground. He was also imprisoned, but soon escaped from jail, and was allowed to remain at large, for the reason that the officers were afraid of him.   His wife soon got a divorce from him; but he was determined to kill Allen, and it was known that on several occasions he had secretly watched for him.   Failing to get a chance at Allen, who was really in hiding, Bean sought a difficulty with Allen's brother, whom he assaulted and beat unmercifully.   For this he was indicted; but, up to the time that court met with Jackson on the bench, the officers had not been able to arrest him, or at all events they had not arrested him. They reported to Judge Jackson that they could not take Bean; that he was out at his cabin, on the south side of the town, armed, sitting constantly, when at home, in the door, with his rifle by his side and his pistols in his lap, defying arrest and threatening to kill the first man who approached his house. Such was the report made in open court to Judge Jackson, who immediately ordered: "Summon every man in the court house, and bring Bean in here dead or alive."   Thereupon the sheriff, with a grim humor which does him infinite credit, responded, "Then I summon your honor first!"   Jackson at once left the bench, exclaiming, "By the Eternal, I'll bring him!"—and he did.   He found Bean sitting in his door, as described by the officers.   Jackson approached, pistol in hand, followed by the crowd at a respectful distance.   When he got within shooting distance, Bean arose, called out, "I'll surrender to you, Mr. Devil!" and laid down his arms.   Jackson took him to the court room, where he was tried and fined heavily.

This is the story of the Bean incident, as always told by the old people in Washington county. Russell Bean was a man of fine appearance and engaging manners. He was not only a genius, but he was "well read" for that era, and had picked up, on his trip to Connecticut and at New Orleans, a great deal of information with reference to other nations and their affairs. He could have been a leader, but for some infirmities and peculiarities.

When Parton was preparing his life of Jackson, some one gave him the information that Col. Charles Roberson, Bean's father-in-law, was "an illiterate old man, who had fought under Sevier at King's Mountain and made campaigns against the Indians." This statement, unqualified, does Col. Roberson injustice. He was one of the heroes of King's Mountain, and had engaged in many campaigns against the Indians. He was not an educated man, but the various responsible positions to which he was appointed, including that of chairman of the Court of Pleas and Quarter Sessions, according to early records at Jonesboro, and speaker of the Senate in the last General Assembly of the State of Franklin, 1787, testify to his intelligence, as well as the esteem and confidence in which he was held by his countrymen.

Bean's divorced wife married again, and moved to Knoxville, where the unfortunate child died, as did also her second husband. In the course of a few years, Bean himself drifted to Knoxville, where Jackson met him and, it is said, brought about a reconciliation between him and his former wife. They were remarried, and lived happily until the death of Bean.

Parton fixes the date of the fire incident at Jonesboro at the time of the Bean incident—after Jackson had been appointed judge. The date is not material, but Parton's information must have been incorrect, or the date of the fire incident, as recollected and given by aged persons who remembered it and recounted it as late as twenty years ago, was wrong. According to these old citizens, the fire in which Jackson distinguished himself was in 1798, while he was stopping in Jonesboro on his way to Nashville from Philadelphia, after he had resigned the position of United States Senator. Court was in session, however, when the fire occurred, as stated by Parton, and Jackson was there mingling with his friends. He had been there for a few days previous to the fire, and continued his stay in town for a few days afterward. He was not stopping at the tavern, but was the guest of one of the families.

The fire originated, near midnight, in the stable that belonged to and was near the Rawlings tavern. It was soon in a blaze throughout, and there was no thought of an effort to save it, as it was filled with hay, oats, fodder, etc. Attention was turned to the tavern, which stood some two hundred and fifty feet from a creek which runs through the center of the town. The alarm of fire and the call for help brought out the entire population, filling the few streets of the village with men, women and children. When Jackson appeared on the scene, Ben Boyd, an Irish coppersmith, was calling loudly for buckets and yelling to the crowd to form a line to the creek; but nobody was paying any attention to him. Jackson, as was his custom, immediately took command, and began ordering everybody to get into line, actually taking hold of men and women and putting them in position, calling for buckets, and directing the keeper of the tavern to get all of the blankets in the house and spread them all over the roof. In a few minutes Jackson had formed two lines from the house to the creek, the lines facing each other and six or eight feet apart; along one line empty buckets were passed to the creek, and the full buckets back up the other line to the tavern, which was the only house in immediate danger. Jackson would appear, one moment, on the roof, calling down to those in the lines to stand firm and hurry up the water, and the tavern and town would be saved; the next seen of him, he would be passing up and down the lines, urging order and discipline. He was everywhere, and always at the place where his presence seemed most needed. The tavern was saved, and nothing burned but the stable. "Jackson saved the town with his bucket brigade," was on every lip.

Parton brings Benjamin Boyd to the attention of the nation, in connection with this fire incident, by saying that, "while Gen. Jackson was strengthening that part of his line near the creek, a drunken coppersmith named Boyd, who said that he had seen fires at Baltimore, began to give orders and annoy persons in the line. Jackson shouted at Boyd to fall in line, who continued jabbering. Jackson seized a bucket by the handle, knocked him down, and walked along the line giving orders as coolly as before." Ben Boyd's part in and connection with the fire incident, as detailed to me "often and again" by persons who knew all the facts, does not agree with Parton's account in some particulars. What is believed to be the true narrative is here given.

Benjamin Boyd was an Irishman, as was Andrew Jackson. He was a coppersmith by trade, got drunk occasionally, and was drunk on the night of the fire. He was somewhat chagrined at the idea of Jackson appropriating his suggestion of a bucket-line to the creek; and after Jackson had succeeded in doing what he could not do, and, as Boyd said, was "strutting around giving orders," the two men met near the creek. Boyd said to Jackson, "I have seen and fought fires in Philadelphia before you were born," and continued to growl at Jackson, who ordered him to "get in line or get out of the way." Boyd, who was a fearless man, made some insolent reply, when Jackson, seizing a bucket of water, threw its contents on the irate Irishman, and passed along the line, leaving Boyd swearing, "By the Holy Virgin, I'll whip you before you leave this town!" John Chester, with whom Boyd lived and died at Jonesboro, made him go to his little house, which stood in the corner of Chester's yard; and this ended the matter. *

"Jackson's bucket brigade" has often saved property in the ancient town, within the century, now almost rounded out, that followed its organization and first service.

* My greatgrandfather, Robert Johnston Chester, brought Benjamin Boyd from Limerick, Ireland, to America. My grandfather, John Chester, brought him from Carlisle, Pennsylvania, to Jonesboro, in December, 1796. Boyd was then an old man. I am the possessor of one of Boyd's books, an "Arithmetick," "printed in Belfast, Ireland, by James Magee, at the Bible and Crown, Bridge street," in 1775.

CHAPTER X.

ANDREW JACKSON was a more courageous man, as well as a much greater man, than many of his most ardent admirers knew of. At the time of his duel with Avery, if the version which I believe to be true is correct, he was afraid of public opinion—that is, he believed that, if he made an explanation, somebody might think that he feared Avery, and so, rather than run the risk of being suspected of cowardice, he was willing to give Avery a chance to kill him. But later in life he had outgrown this, and had no master except his convictions of duty, his own sense of right and wrong. He did not care what anybody might believe or suspect him of, so long as his course had the approval of his judgment and his conscience.

This was established beyond doubt, in the minds of a few old gentlemen (who afterward learned the actual facts), by an incident which happened in 1832—probably in the early part of October—at the public house or tavern kept by Capt. Bell at Bean's Station, in Grainger county. President Jackson had left Washington, in the early part of August, 1832, in company with Francis P. Blair and others, to visit the Hermitage; and the incident about to be related occurred on the return trip to Washington. Before leaving the Hermitage, the itinerary or schedule of travel and stopping-places on the route had been made out. Bell's tavern had been fixed upon as a point for dinner and rest, and Capt. Bell had been notified of the date. Bell had been a friend and admirer of Jackson for many years,

and he and his wife naturally made great preparations to receive and entertain the President and his accompanying friends.
Quite a number of leading citizens, acquaintances and adherents of Jackson, who had been apprised of the day he would
arrive, were on hand to greet their old friend and leader, the
President of the United States.

The party arrived on time, and the President's carriage
stopped in the public road in front of the tavern, which stood
at some little distance back from the highway. Capt. Bell
and others were at the carriage door to receive President Jackson, who got out immediately and "shook hands all round."
Bell, however, observed that Jackson, with an ominous storm-
cloud gathering on his face, was looking intently toward a
broad porch which extended along the front of the tavern, his
eyes evidently fixed upon a gentleman who was walking back
and forth on this porch, and who was evidently in turn eyeing
Jackson with equal intensity. Suddenly, Jackson turned toward the conveyances which were accompanying him with
friends, some of whom had already gotten out, and said,
"Don't get out—we will not take dinner here." Then, turning to Capt. Bell, he said, "I regret that I can't stop, rest
awhile and take dinner with you. Tell Mrs. Bell that I could
not stop." The latter remark was made in an undertone to
Capt. Bell, after which President Jackson got into his carriage
and ordered his driver to go on, and his friends followed.

Capt. Bell's curiosity was as great as his disappointment at
the turn things had taken. He did not know what had caused
it, but suspected that the presence of the gentleman walking
on the porch had something, if not everything, to do with it.
This gentleman had only stopped for dinner, and left immediately after it was over, without alluding to the Jackson incident. Indeed, no one then knew whether or not he knew who

Jackson was; but Capt. Bell, during the hour or so that he remained, learned what afterward proved to be three important facts—the name of the gentleman, that he was from North Carolina, and that he was on his way to Kentucky. At that time, the thoroughfare from all East Tennessee, North Carolina, South Carolina and Georgia was by way of Bean's Station through Cumberland Gap to Kentucky.

Some months later, Capt. Bell learned that the gentleman in question was one of President Jackson's most bitter and unrelenting enemies; that he was in fact the leader of the opposition to Jackson in North Carolina; that he had made public speeches in North Carolina and elsewhere against him, in the campaigns of 1824 and 1828, and was then (1832) most active in his opposition; and that he was at that time probably on his way to Kentucky to consult with Jackson's opponents in that state. He, as Bell afterwards learned, had rehashed in his public speeches all the slanders which had been invented against Jackson, including no doubt the one which had cost Dickinson his life in 1806. After learning these facts, Capt. Bell said that he well knew the terrific struggle which Jackson had then and there, to control the storm rising within his breast as he saw, within a few yards of him, a hated foe who had committed a crime which, in Jackson's judgment, ought to bar him out of heaven. But Bell's idea was that Jackson—the man with a temper like a tornado, and whose very nature, as some professed to believe, was nothing but a raging torrent of fury— said to himself, "I am President of the United States; and I can not afford to bring reproach upon the people who elected me, or to degrade the highest office on earth by a scene, or a difficulty with that man, which is certain to follow if I stop here"; and he therefore immediately got into his carriage, and left without any explanation except the words given above.

When Capt. Bell met Jackson again, a few years afterward, no explanation was necessary—he knew all.

Capt. Bell's son, who as a young man was present when the incident occurred, is authority for the account given above, and for his father's views and recollections of it. So far as I know, it has not been published hitherto.

Those who knew Andrew Jackson would agree with Bell that it took a superhuman effort even to remember, at the moment, that he was President of the United States, and to control the passion that the sight of this man aroused in him; but he did it, and, in doing it, proved himself a greater man, if possible, than many of his friends ever believed him to be. The struggle that the President of the United States had with Andrew Jackson, on this occasion, can better be understood when it is remembered that the man walking on the porch had repeated statements which, it is said, was the origin of Jackson's trouble with Sevier and others, and which also caused Jackson, in his duel with Dickinson, after the latter had fired and hit him, to place his left hand tightly on the spot where the ball had entered, take deliberate aim with the other hand and pull the trigger; and then, when the weapon failed to fire, the hammer having caught at the half-cock notch, to examine it carefully, recock it, aim carefully again, and fire again—this time to see his enemy fall mortally wounded, dying in a few moments afterward. Jackson's act at Bean's Station, in leaving abruptly the presence of a calumniator of the memory of the wife whom he had worshipped in life, and at the very mention of whose name after her death tears came into his eyes and a tremor in his voice, was an exhibition of courage and self-control showing greatness in a direction and to a degree not often met with in the very greatest of great men.

On this same journey from Washington to the Hermitage, in

1832, President Jackson was given an ovation and reception which, it is believed, was the most pleasing and gratifying to him of any of the numerous public demonstrations of popular esteem theretofore shown him. This affair had its beginning four miles northeast of Jonesboro, on the public highway—the old state road—on each side of which, at the point mentioned, was an old-fashioned crooked rail fence, and also large oak and other native forest trees. It was in the latter part of August, or early in September, and the day was an ideal one. The road was on and along the top of a high ridge, with the Iron Mountain in plain view across the valley to the south. At this point, the President was met by one hundred picked men, uniformed, and mounted on a hundred of the very finest dapple-grey saddle horses that could be found in the country, to escort him into Jonesboro. This column of horsemen was under command of Samuel Greer, a life-long friend of Jackson. As it approached the carriage of the President, who had had no intimation of its approach, and got within about a hundred feet, a hundred stentorian voices simultaneously shouted: "Three cheers for Andrew Jackson, the greatest man on earth!" and the cheers which followed made the welkin ring and woke the echoes of three commonwealths.

The carriage was pulled to the right of the road, under the shade of a large oak (which was still standing as late as 1884), and the President alighted, removing his hat as he did so, and bowing three several times to the horsemen. This act of course caused another burst of applause. When quiet was restored, the column, at the command of Greer, dismounted and passed to the rear, where he introduced each one to the President. It is said that the latter, in as many as forty or more instances, while holding some young man by the hand, would tell him who his mother was before her marriage, what

9

his father's given name was, and in what part of the county he had lived—whether on Watauga, Nolichucky or Holston river, or on Limestone, Cherokee, Boon's, Brush or Knob creek. After this, Jackson turned in the direction of the Iron Mountain, and as he pointed to it, said in substance: "Forty-four years ago last spring, I crossed that mountain, and settled, as I then thought, in this country permanently, amongst your fathers and ancestors; but Providence had decreed that I should not spend my life in this particular part of our great state, and took me elsewhere. Every time, for the last few days, that my carriage has been where I could see that mountain, I have been looking out at it, and letting my mind run back over my stormy and eventful life; and, at the moment you approached and gave me the first notice I had of your coming by your cheers and applause, I was thinking of whom I would meet and whom I would miss of my old friends at the old town just ahead of us, where I began life. I wish to say, before we resume the journey to the town, that in all my career I have not been the recipient of a demonstration more greatly appreciated than this one, here under the old trees, in this old road that I used to travel so often, by the sons of my old friends and acquaintances." Then, with Greer and ten of the escort some little distance in front of the carriage, and ninety in the rear, the journey was resumed. It was understood throughout the country that Jackson would arrive in Jonesboro that afternoon, and also that he would spend the next day in the old town. This had brought thousands of people to Jonesboro; men, women and children came, on foot, on horseback and in every kind of vehicle. There was no way to house and feed the multitude that had arrived and filled the town when Jackson reached it late in the afternoon. The sides of the road were lined with people for a mile outside the town, the

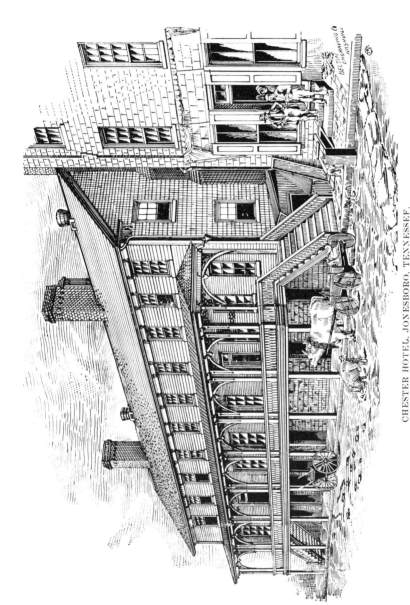

CHESTER HOTEL, JONESBORO, TENNESSEE.

On the porch of which Jackson held the reception in 1832. From a photograph taken in 1881.

streets were packed, the tops of many of the houses were covered, and the President was received with waving of hats, bonnets, aprons, handkerchiefs and improvised flags and with shouts from the multitude, from the time he came in sight until he got out of his carriage and went into the hotel.

The hotel at which he stopped was on the main street, and had a broad porch that extended the full length of the house. This was about eight or ten feet high, projecting out over the sidewalk, and was reached by a stairway at each end. On the following day, the President held a reception on this porch, and there shook hands with all of the people who had assembled to see him, they passing up at one end of the porch and down at the other. On this porch, on this day, was dispelled from the minds of some of his friends every vestige of the slight suspicion which had been produced by vile hired slanderers, that his fierce nature, turbulent spirit and stormy life had sapped his mental powers, judgment and reason, and that he was no longer the real Andrew Jackson of New Orleans, but was surrounded and controlled by designing, unscrupulous scoundrels, who were feeding the vanity of the old man in his dotage on flattery which he was then unable to detect and resist. President Jackson stood on the hotel porch at Jonesboro, and, possibly at the very moment when public speakers and editors in other parts of the country were lamenting(?) the loss of his former ''energy of character'' and the decay of his mind and judgment, gave to those people the very highest evidence that he was the Andrew Jackson of old: his form, although he was sixty-five years old, was ''straight as a gunbarrel,'' and his eyes as flashing and his mind as clear as on the night of the fire, or on the day when he left the bench and arrested Russell Bean, in that very town. As his old friends would approach him in their plain and simple garb, with their wives and children,* he would call out their names, grasp their hands, put an arm around them, kiss their daughters, compliment their younger children, and tell the wife that the good-looking boys and girls "favored her" more than they did the father.   Incidents of his early life would suggest themselves to his mind—a lawsuit, a fox chase, a deer drive or something else—as they came up, and he would refer to it in some way, in the few moments which he could spare to that particular individual.   His famous horse-race with Col. Love in Greasy Cove was mentioned; and it came very near bringing down the porch when a kinsman of Col. Love, by the same name, grasped the old hero by the hand and asked him if he had any better race horses at the Hermitage than he had when he lived in that country; to which he promptly and laughingly replied: "Yes, better than either one of us had that day; come over to the Hermitage, and you shall have one."   Such were the scenes and incidents of that memorable day on the hotel porch in the historic old town of Jonesboro.†

The "bank conspirators," as they were called, had been at work incessantly, and they had a few—a very few—helpers in that country, who had been furnished with and had repeated

---

* During the progress of this reception, on the porch of the old Chester Hotel, a lady—an old friend and admirer of Jackson—came up to him, and after a cordial greeting, she presented her little son and namesake of the President. President Jackson was so impressed with the manner and appearance of the little fellow, that he gave him a "five-dollar gold piece." This little fellow grew up to manhood, became a teacher and then a lawyer. During the late war he was Lieutenant Colonel of the 8th Tennessee Federal Cavalry; then a State Senator some years ago from the first district; then Circuit Judge of the First judicial circuit, which position he held for eight years; now resides at Greeneville, Tenn., an honored and respected lawyer, citizen and gentleman, and still has the five-dollar gold piece—Hon. Andrew Jackson Brown.

† My mother, whose maiden name was Mary M. Chester, married for her first husband Richard Gammon, Jr., and they resided at Blountville, Sullivan county, where Jackson was their guest on this trip from Washington, for the night preceding his arrival at Jonesboro. Mr. Gammon and my mother accompanied the President from Blountville to Jonesboro, where my mother was born and reared, and she was present on the hotel porch during this reception.

(with great regret?) this charge of imbecility of old age, which rendered it dangerous to the liberties of the people and perilous to the government to re-elect the once great man, then a mental wreck. It may, even at this late day, be of benefit to reproduce in part an editorial from one of the newspapers of the period—a strong and powerful one—which, it was said, had been hired to desert and slander President Jackson, and to wait until he was in the midst of his journey through the country to the Hermitage, before it made its first assault on him. This editorial, among other things, said:

Since 1823 I have been the firm, undeviating friend of Andrew Jackson, through good and through evil report. I have defended his reputation and advocated his cause; and, for the last five years, my exertions in his behalf, as the conductor of a public journal, have been known to this country. But the time has now arrived when I owe it to the people, to the institutions of the country and to myself to declare my deliberate conviction that he has not realized the high hopes which his reputation and previously written and declared opinions promised, nor redeemed the sacred pledges which he voluntarily gave on his election to the first station in the world. Let us not be misunderstood: I do not—I never will—impeach his patriotism or his integrity; but as a sentinel at my post, true to the duty which I voluntarily assumed when I became the editor of a public journal, I feel called upon to proclaim to the people that Andrew Jackson is not their President; that, enfeebled by age and the toils, cares and anxieties of an active and laborious life, he no longer possesses his former energy of character or independence of mind, but, confiding in those who have wormed themselves into his confidence, he has entrusted the affairs of this great nation and the happiness of thirteen millions of freemen to the hands of political gamblers and money-changers, time-serving politicians, who, in the pursuit of their unhallowed purposes, threaten ruin to the country and to that sacred charter of our liberties which was maintained by the wisdom of our fathers, after having been purchased with their blood and the sacrifice of every selfish motive on the altar of public good.*

* New York *Courier and Enquirer*, quoted by Parton, III, 428.

The foregoing is from a three-column editorial which appeared during the very week that Jackson was in Jonesboro, and only about two days previous to his reception in that town. Eight newspapers that had theretofore supported Jackson immediately followed the lead of the *Courier and Enquirer*, took the names of Jackson and Van Buren from their mast-heads, and went over to the support of Nicholas Biddle and the banks, on the ground that the President had lost his mind and his "former energy of character"; but they all lived long enough to find out how the people of Jonesboro received the slander, * and also to learn that the whole country knew that they had been hired to traduce the life, character, abilities and public services of this great soldier, statesman and patriot, and to have the finger of indignant, honest scorn point them out as traitors to the cause and slanderers of Andrew Jackson.

Space has been given to this reception at Jonesboro for the reason that it took place during the period of ten days within which nine or ten of the newspapers in the east which had been supporting Jackson suddenly discovered that he had "lost his former energy of character and independence of mind," and was so "enfeebled by age" that his re-election would endanger the happiness of the people and the "sacred charter of liberty." This was nothing more nor less than the first move in the conspiracy that was formed to defeat his re-election and destroy him. These newspapers had been bought, the price paid and the trade closed, some time after Jackson's nomination on the 21st of May preceding, at Baltimore; but they were instructed to reserve their opening fire upon him until an opportune time. It was ascertained that he was about to visit the Hermitage, and that he was going "overland" down across Virginia and

---

*The *Courier and Enquirer* which contained this editorial, reaching Jonesboro a few days after Jackson's reception, was torn in pieces, trampled and burned in the street.

on through Tennessee. When he was about midway on this journey, with no telegraph or fast mail communication to give him information, these "bushwhackers" fired on his character, his integrity and his administration, and yet protested in the same editorials that they did not intend to "impeach his patriotism or his integrity."

The cold-blooded, savage brutality of this conspiracy; its "lying in wait," concealment in ambush for weeks, to catch the victim away from home, out in the interior on a long journey, and then assault and attempt to assassinate his character, is without parallel in American political warfare. But the people could not be bought, deceived, driven nor intimidated. Of the popular vote cast in the election, that year, Jackson received 687,502, and Clay 530,189. Jackson carried seventeen out of twenty-four states, and received 219 out of 288 electoral votes.

If the men who became the tools of this conspiracy to ruin his usefulness, and to cloud his former fair name and fame, had any sensibilities left, what must have been the depth of their humiliation when, in June, 1833, Andrew Jackson, then President of the United States for a second term, and sixty-six years of age, rode on horseback along Broadway in the city of New York. Parton describes it in a few words:

And what a scene was that, when the Old Man, victorious over nullification, and about to deal his finishing blow at the bank, visited New York, and was borne along Broadway on one roaring wave of upturned faces and flashing eyes; when it seemed, said a spectator, as if he had but to speak the word, and they would have proclaimed him on the spot a king.*

This ovation in New York was after he had been elected; the other mentioned was before he was elected, and was given

* Life, preface.

to *the man,* in a country road, between crooked rail fences, under the shade of the native oaks.

President Jackson, during his second term, carried out his "previously written and declared opinions and promises," and "redeemed the sacred pledges which he voluntarily gave," by crushing the United States Banks and freeing the people, commerce and trade from their domination, bringing shame and disgrace upon the conspirators and the hired traducers of this great man, whose name and fame will not perish until the departed spirit of American Independence shall shake hands with the ghost of Liberty across the grave of the greatest republic that has ever existed.

A CENTENNIAL DREAM.

BY DR. R. L. C. WHITE.

(Nashville American, March 7, 1897.)

HAVING spent an afternoon in wandering about the Centennial grounds, I had devoted the evening to Haywood, Ramsey and other chroniclers of early Tennessee history. These two circumstances combined were doubtless the cause of a singular dream which I had that night. I thought that I stood in the Auditorium, and saw congregated within its walls many of the famous men and women of the past whose names are closely interwoven with the history of our state. They seemed to constitute a convention of some kind ; and, although the assemblage had not yet been called to order, the chair had already been taken, very appropriately, by the illustrious patriot whom Andrew Jackson styled ''the Father of Tennessee'' (1), while the publisher of the first newspaper issued in the state (2) acted as secretary, assisted by the first native historian of Tennessee (3), the founder of the first ''campaign paper'' established west of the Alleghanies (4), and the editor of the first abolition paper issued in the south (5).

Seated upon the platform were several persons who seemed to have been designated as vice presidents of the meeting. There were the statesman who defeated another eminent Tennessean for speaker of the national House of Representatives, and was in turn defeated by him (6); the only two United States Senators from Tennessee who were ever expelled (7, 8); the only Confederate States Senators from Tennessee (9, 10); the man of whom an ex-President of the United States said that he was "the greatest natural orator in Congress" (11); the United States Senator who published the first map of Tennessee (12); "Old Bullion" (13); and the patriot who, on resigning his seat in the Senate because he could not conscientiously obey the instructions of the legislature, said: "For myself, I am proud that my state can, in my person, yet produce one man willing to be made a sacrifice rather than sacrifice his principles" (14).

An interesting quartet, near the stage, consisted of the member of the first constitutional convention who proposed the name "Tennessee" for the infant commonwealth (15); the eminent statesman who said of the first constitution of Tennessee that it was "the least imperfect and most republican" of any which had been adopted up to that time (16); and the presidents respectively of the second and third constitutional conventions (17, 18).

Seated together, a little farther back, were the two men who signed the act ceding "the territory south of the Ohio" to the United States (19, 20); the Virginia statesman in whose honor, at the suggestion of Andrew Jackson, a county was named, in recognition of his earnest advocacy of the admission of Tennessee to the Union (21); the man who gave in the Senate the casting vote which secured that admission (22); and the commissioner who was sent by the Confederate government to effect the withdrawal of Tennessee from the Union (23).

Chatting pleasantly together, in one corner of the hall, was a notable group of women, comprising the wife of whom her husband left the record that she was "a being so gentle and yet so virtuous, slander might wound, but could not dishonor" (24);

the only female for whom a Tennessee county has ever been named (25); the pioneer maiden who, in endeavoring to escape from Indians, fell into the arms of the soldier who afterwards became her husband (26); and the beautiful Irish girl who was the cause of the disruption of a President's cabinet (27); while near them "the Pocahontas of the West" (28) stood silently listening.

A remarkable group was composed of the famous general whose name was bestowed on the largest area ever embraced within the limits of a single county (29); a nobleman whose ancestral name, in abbreviated form, is borne by a Tennessee county (30); the explorer who named the Cumberland mountains and riv· (31); the governor by whose misspelled name a large part of Tennessee was known for many years (32); the revolutionary soldier in whose honor the first settlement on the Cumberland was called (33); and the famous explorer whose mysterious death, within the limits of the county which now bears his name, has never been satisfactorily explained (34).

A picturesque trio consisted of the leader of the first body of white men who ever set foot on the soil of Tennessee (35); the first white man who erected an edifice within its limits (36); and the nobleman whose titular name was given to the first structure built therein by English-speaking people (37).

Grouped modestly in the rear of the hall were several men whose dress and accoutrements proclaimed them pioneers. There were the famous "big-foot hunter" who lived in a hollow tree (38); the man whom the Indians called the "fool warrior" on account of his reckless bravery (39); the commander of a marvellous expedition by water, of which it has been said that "it has no parallel in modern history" (40); the man for whom the oldest town in the state was named (41); the first white child born in Tennessee (42); the first white

child born in Nashville (43); and the bridegroom of the first
marriage ceremony performed west of the Cumberland mountains (44).

Just beyond these, leaning on their Deckhard rifles, stood
three men who would have attracted attention anywhere—the
celebrated backwoodsman who left an engraved record to desig-
nate the spot where he had "cilled a bar" (45); another, equally
famous, who relates in his autobiography that he killed one
hundred and five bears in less than a year (46); and still another who shot thirty-two of these "varmints" during one
winter within seven miles of Nashville (47).

I was much interested in the appearance of a number of in-
telligent-looking men who sat together, engaged in earnest conversation.   There were the man who founded the first educational
institution in the Mississippi valley (48); the first minister who
preached regularly to a Tennessee congregation (49); the bishop
whose journal forms a valuable contribution to the history of
early times in this state (50); the president of the first non-
sectarian college chartered in the United States (51); the classmate of Daniel Webster who founded the first academy for females in Tennessee (52); and the eminent educator who declined
successively the presidency of seven universities and colleges
in other states, in order that he might continue his chosen work
in this (53).

Immediately in rear of these were the illustrious savant
who first mapped the Gulf Stream, and demonstrated the fea-
sibility of a submarine cable (54); the first state geologist of
Tennessee (55); a distinguished surgeon who served profession-
ally in the armies of three countries (56); and the young phy-
sician who, while perishing in a snow-storm on Mont Blanc,
kept a record of his sensations for the benefit of science (57).

Just across the aisle sat the first chief justice of Tennessee

(58); the judge who, after having been chief justice of Kentucky, removed to this state and became the greatest criminal advocate in the history of its bar (59); the first judge who was ever impeached in Tennessee (60); the eminent jurist who wrote President Jackson's farewell address (61); and the judge whose singular death from the attack of an infuriated turkey-gobbler was regarded by the early settlers as retributive justice for official oppression (62).

A literary group was composed of "the father of Tennessee history" (63); the famous printer whose name a short-lived commonwealth once bore (64); the English author who founded a colony in this state which was named for the scene of his best-known book (65); a Tennessee editor who was afterward elected to a seat in the British parliament (66); the author of "Hymns to the Gods" (67); and "Sut Lovengood" (68).

In a prominent position in the center of the hall were a man who was governor of two states of the Union (69); a governor of Tennessee who was buried in two states (70); the first man who became governor by virtue of his position as speaker of the Senate (71); one who was elected governor, but never inaugurated (72); a governor who was presented by a grand jury as a public nuisance (73); one to whom a celebrated author referred as having given to his official station "the ill-savor of a corner grocery" (74); the only person present at the death of Henry Clay except the members of his immediate household (75); the editor famous as "the fighting parson" (76); and the man who, by casting the entire vote of the state at a national convention, although he was merely a chance by-stander, gave a new word to Tennessee politics (77).

A distinguished looking body was composed of the revolutionary general to whom 25,000 acres of land in Tennessee were granted by legislative enactment (78); a famous fighter under Jackson who was said to have been "a great general without knowing it" (79) ; a naval officer who was master of a vessel at twelve years of age, and whom one of the best-known of American poets has styled

"The sea-king of the sovereign west
Who made his mast a throne" (80);

the Tennessee postmaster to whom Andrew Jackson bequeathed a sword (81); the colonel of the famous "Bloody First" (82); and the "grey-eyed man of destiny" (83).

Elsewhere were to be seen the man who supplied the funds which equipped John Sevier for King's Mountain (84); the man who furnished Jackson all the cannon-balls used by him at New Orleans (85); the first man who coined silver money in Tennessee (86); the owner of the first steamboat that ever landed at Nashville (87); the man who inaugurated the movement for building the first railroad in Tennessee, and was long known as "Old Chattanooga" in consequence (88); the man who exchanged a cow and calf for the hill on which the state capitol was afterwards built (89); the man who bought the ground on which a large part of one of the most important cities in the state now stands, for a rifle, a mare and a pair of leather breeches (90); the discoverer of the Yosemite valley (91); the famous philanthropist who was chiefly instrumental in the founding of a state asylum for the insane (92); the author of the first bill for the establishment of a normal school in Tennessee (93) ; and the patriotic citizen who erected, at his own expense, the first monument to the memory of John Sevier (94).

A striking pair was composed of the man in whose veins circulated the blood of four races, and who simultaneously held commissions in the armies of three countries and was loyal to none (95); and the Choctaw chief who was graduated at the University of Nashville, and of whom Charles Dickens has said that he was "as stately and complete a gentleman, of nature's making," as he had ever met (96). Another pair, quite as striking, consisted of the first permanent settler at French Lick (97), conversing volubly in his own tongue with a royal personage who visited Nashville in his youth, and afterwards became a king (98).

Just then the presiding officer arose and gave a premonitory rap with his gavel. As he did so, I saw slipping furtively out of a rear door "the great western land pirate" (99), closely followed by the man who was instrumental in bringing him to justice (100).

INTERPRETATION OF THE "DREAM."

(Nashville American, May 16, 1897.)

1. James Robertson.
2. George Roulstone.
3. James Gattys McGregor Ramsey.
4. Allen Anderson Hall.
5. Elihu Embree.
6. John Bell.
7. William Blount.
8. Alfred Osborn Pope Nicholson.
9. Landon Carter Haynes.
10. Gustavus Adolphus Henry.
11. Meredith Poindexter Gentry.
12. Daniel Smith.
13. Thomas Hart Benton.
14. Hugh Lawson White.
15. Andrew Jackson.

16. Thomas Jefferson.
17. William Blount Carter.
18. John Calvin Brown.
19. Charles Johnson.
20. Stephen Cabarrus.
21. William Branch Giles.
22. Samuel Livermore.
23. Henry Washington Hilliard.
24. Rachel Jackson.
25. Mary Grainger.
26. Catharine (or Katherine) Sherrill.
27. Margaret O'Neill (or O'Neal).
28. Nancy Ward.
29. George Washington.
30. Marie Jean Paul Roche Yves Gilbert Motier de Lafayette.
31. Thomas Walker.
32. Estevan Miro.
33. Francis Nash.
34. Meriwether Lewis.
35. Fernando (or Ferdinand or Hernando) DeSoto.
36. Robert Cavelier de La Salle.
37. John Campbell, Earl of Loudoun.
38. Thomas Sharpe (or Sharp) Spencer.
39. Abraham Castleman.
40. John Donelson.
41. Willie Jones.
42. Russell Bean.
43. Felix Robertson.
44. James Leiper (or Leeper).
45. Daniel Boone (or Boon).
46. David Crockett.
47. John Rains.

48. Samuel Doak.
49. Tidence Lane.
50. Francis Asbury.
51. Samuel Carrick.
52. Moses Fisk (or Fiske).
53. Philip Lindsley.
54. Matthew Fontaine Maury.
55. Gerard Troost.
56. Paul Fitzsimmons Eve.
57. James Baxter Bean.
58. John Catron.
59. Felix Grundy.
60. David Campbell.
61. Roger Brooke Taney.
62. Samuel Spencer.
63. John Haywood.
64. Benjamin Franklin.
65. Thomas Hughes.
66. John Mitchel.
67. Albert Pike.
68. George Washington Harris.
69. Samuel Houston.
70. John Sevier.
71. William Hall.
72. Robert Looney Caruthers.
73. James Knox Polk.
74. Andrew Johnson.
75. James Chamberlain Jones.
76. William Gannaway Brownlow.
77. Edmund Rucker.
78. Nathanael (or Nathaniel) Greene.
79. John Coffee.

10

80. David Glasgow (or Glascoe) Farragut.

81. Robert Armstrong.

82. William Bowen Campbell.

83. William Walker.

84. John Adair.

85. Montgomery Bell.

86. Charles Roberson.

87. William Carroll.

88. James Overton.

89. George Washington Campbell.

90. David Shelby.

91. Joseph Reddeford Walker.

92. Dorothea Lynde Dix.

93. Robert Hatton.

94. Albigence Waldo Putnam.

95. Alexander McGillivray (or McGilveray).

96. Peter P. Pitchlynn.

97. Timote (or Timothy) Demonbreun.

98. Louis Philippe.

99. John Arnold Murrell.

100. Virgil Adam Stewart.

In the matter of the orthography of the foregoing names, lattitude is allowed wherever it is proper to do so. For example, the famous "backwoodsman of Kentucky" was in the habit of signing his name "Boon" or "Boone," as the fancy struck him; Capt. Leiper was known as "Leiper" or "Leeper" indifferently, the latter having been the signature to the Cumberland Compact; the surname of "Bonnie Kate" is always printed as "Sherrill" by historians (the "Sherril" of Putnam being manifestly a typographical error), although her father wrote his name "Sherrell"; that romantic scoundrel, Alexander McGillivray, was almost as versatile in the matter of autographic variants of his family name as was Shakespeare—Capt. Allison, in his "Dropped Stitches in Tennessee History," speaks of having examined two autograph letters, one of which is signed "McGillivray" and the other "McGilveray"; the middle name of the "big foot hunter" is "Sharpe" or "Sharp," as may be; the Moses Fisk of history appears in the catalog of Dartmouth College as "Fiske"; and while the actual name of the "pretty Peggy" of Jackson's time seems unquestionably to have been Margaret O'Neill, Parton invariably prints it "O'Neal." On the other hand, there are several cases in which it is not at all difficult to determine the absolutely accurate orthography. Instances are the Christian name of Meriwether Lewis, a facsimile of whose autograph may be found in Appleton's "Cyclopedia of American Biography," and who invariably signed his name as it is here given, although the Tennessee legislature, with that faculty for blundering which seems an inevitable characteristic of Tennessee legislatures at all periods, inscribed his tombstone "Merriwether"; the Earl of Loudoun, for any other spelling of whose name there is no shadow of authority; John Mitchel, the Irish patriot; Willie (pronounced "Wylie") Jones, whose Christian name many persons seem to regard as a diminutive of "William" (even Phelan makes this error); Demonbreun, which is the form the name of the pioneer of French Lick assumed when its bearer, who was "De Mont Breun" in France, came to America—the various curious shapes in which the name is given by Haywood and Ramsey being merely vagaries of the fancy of these worthies, who had an ingenuous habit, where proper names were concerned, of "spelling by ear"; and notably the "misspelled name" referred to in 32, which, given by Haywood, Ramsey and Putnam in various forms (all of them incorrect), is rightly given in Martin's history of Louisiana—unquestionable authority in all matters relating to that period. A photographic reproduction of Miro's autograph signature may be found in a recent issue of that valuable publication, Professor Garrett's "Magazine of American History." One name which is incorrectly printed in all the histories is that of Charles Roberson.   Capt. John Allison informs me that the old court records at Jonesboro show that he invariably signed his name as I have given it above. It may be well here to state that the general belief that Charles Roberson was a relative of Gen. James Robertson is incorrect.

In connection with the identity of the editor referred to in 4, attention may here properly be called to a remarkable blunder in Crew's History of Nashville, where the positive assertion is made that Jeremiah George Harris, in 1840, "issued the first campaign paper ever issued west of the Alleghanies, named *Advance Guard of the Democracy*, and this occasioned the issue from the office of the *Banner* of *The Spirit of '76*, a Whig campaign paper." This statement is the exact reverse of the fact, the first issue of *The Spirit of '76* (Allen A. Hall's paper) having made its appearance March 14, 1840, while Harris's paper did not see the light until the 23d of the following April, it having evidently been suggested by, instead of suggesting, the rival campaign paper. This blunder is the more singular from the fact that bound volumes of both papers were easily accessible to the writer in the library of the Tennessee Historical Society—and he does not even give the name of Harris's paper correctly !

There can be no doubt that Elihu Embree was really the first abolition editor. To settle definitely a matter which all of the histories and biographical dictionaries (so far as I have examined, without exception) misstate—they invariably call Benjamin Lundy the pioneer in anti-slavery journalism—I quote here a passage from an extremely rare book—Lundy's

Autobiography.   After narrating his experiences in St. Louis, in
1819, which caused his determination to return to his home in
Ohio, Lundy says: "Before I left St. Louis I heard that Elihu
Embree had commenced the publication of an anti-slavery paper called 'The Emancipator' at Jonesborough, in Tennessee;
but on my way home I was informed of the death of Embree,
and I determined immediately to establish a periodical of my
own.   I therefore removed to Mount Pleasant [Ohio] and
commenced the publication of 'The Genius of Universal Emancipation,' in January, 1821.   .   .   .   When the friends of
the deceased Embree heard of my paper they urged me to remove to Tennessee and use the press on which his had been
printed.   I assented, and after having issued eight monthly
numbers of the 'Genius' I started for Tennessee.   On my arrival I rented the printing office and immediately went to work
with the paper."

Careless reading of Ramsey has led astray a large number
of people with regard to the minister referred to in 49.   Speak-
ing of the expedition of Col. Christian for the relief of the
Watauga settlers in 1772, Ramsey says: "The Rev. Charles
Cummings accompanied the expedition as chaplain, and was
thus the first Christian minister that ever preached in Tennessee."   Granted—but while this is doubtless true, the question
is not who "first preached in Tennessee," but who first
"preached regularly to a Tennessee congregation," and that
this was Tidence Lane, in 1779, is clearly demonstrated elsewhere by Ramsey.   Goodspeed, indeed, using Ramsey's facts,
but changing his language, asserts in terms that Cummings
had charge of a congregation "within the limits of the state";
but Goodspeed is in error in this, as he is in very many other
statements.   In Park's "Historical Discourse," a work which
is the result of the most careful and painstaking original

research, the statement is explicitly made that the congregation to which Goodspeed refers as having enjoyed the ministrations of Cummings ''in the Holston valley as early as 1772,'' was really not located in Tennessee at all. It was ''in Virginia, near the site of the present town of Abingdon.'' Dr. Park, himself a Presbyterian, would not be likely to fail to claim for a minister of his own denomination any credit justly due him.

In order to be absolutely frank, I desire to correct an error— the only one, I believe, in the ''Dream,'' and one fortunately of little moment. The man who ''founded the first academy for females in Tennessee '' (52) was not a classmate of Daniel Webster, as stated ; although the misstatement was made on what I considered good authority.

R. L. C. WHITE.

INDEX.